DORSET
CUSTOMS, CURIOSITIES & COUNTRY LORE

Mary Brown

Ensign
PUBLICATIONS

Published in 1990 by
Ensign Publications
2 Redcar St
Southampton, SO1 5LL

Typeset by Robert Antony Limited, Ringwood.
Edited by David Graves.

ISBN 1 85455 047 0

British Library Cataloguing in Publication Data
Brown, Mary
Dorset: Customs, curiosities and country Lore.
1. Dorset. Social life, history
I. Title
942.33

The Author

Mary Brown began her career as a freelance writer in 1987, after working as a tutor and organiser in Adult Education for students with special needs. She writes regularly for a wide range of local and national publications on a variety of subjects, including the countryside and plants, local history, myths and legends, old customs, folklore and the early Church. This is her first full-length book. Mary has four daughters and a growing number of grandchildren. She lives with her husband at St Leonards, just inside the Dorset border. She was born just outside the Dorset border, in South Somerset, but has strong family connections in various parts of the county. Her main hobby is reading, but she also enjoys drawing, gardening and walking.

Acknowledgements

Special thanks are due to my husband Ken, who took all the present-day photographs and who also read the proofs and gave much moral support. Many other people have helped towards this book and deserve a special mention. John Newth, Editor of Dorset County magazine, for writing the Preface and for giving encouragement to a new and struggling writer. Ruth Allen and June Scammell of Ringwood Library, always ready to help, and who will go to great lengths to track down whatever obscure titles I request. Herbert Elmes, Bailiff of Wareham Court Leet, for information and the loan of photographs. Stan Bartlett of Trent, my Uncle Jack's brother, and Winnie Bartlett, also of Trent, my aunt (widow of Jack) both of whom gave their reminiscences of Dorset long ago.

The following people very kindly helped by providing illustrations. Bill Pearn of Ferndown. Peter Trim of Portland. Ruth Dudley of Westbury. Mr Welch of St Walburga's School, Bournemouth. Mr Armitage of Letchworth, gave permission for use of illustrations from his late father's work, 'Man at Play' published by Frederick Warne 1977. Clinton Grassby of Blandford gave permission for use of a drawing by the late Edward Grassby. Last but by no means least, Brian Marlow of the Memory Lane Picture Company, Parkstone, who has devoted much time to helping with the illustrations. Efforts have been made to trace the copyright holders of all the illustrations used in this book, if we have inadvertently infringed any others we beg their indulgence.

Preface

'DON'T you ever run short of material?' is probably the question I am asked most often in my capacity as Editor of *Dorset County Magazine*. My usual reply is 'That's the least of my problems' because there can be few counties richer than Dorset in fascinating material for the historian, the folklorist, the naturalist.

The material may indeed be plentiful and fascinating, but I know all too well that not everyone has the gift of writing about it. Mary Brown definitely has. Her elegantly clear style, her graphic powers of description, her lightly-worn learning and her ability to bring a story to life make her a regular and distinguished contributor to *Dorset County Magazine*. This, her first full-length book, is a most welcome event.

Folklore is as necessary to the cultural life of a society as food, shelter and warmth are to its physical life. In fact, much folklore has its roots in those physical needs. Some customs, like corn dollies (page 28) and maypoles (page 38), were an expression of hope that the land would bear fruitfully during the coming year. Some were intended to protect the home against evil spirits or more tangible calamity.

Fire, that agent for good that can so easily become an uncontrollable disaster, crops up regularly in folklore; more recent history, as recounted on page 20, shows this to be sadly well-founded pre-occupation. Water (page 74) had connotations both of saving life and of having a life of its own.

Perhaps the most interesting of all folklore's roots lies in Man's atavistic need to fear something he does not understand. Magic, as the chapter on page 70 shows, was a source of fear: wizards, far from being benevolent old gentlemen with long white beards and pointed hats, were next-door to the devil, while the lynching of a suspected witch was motivated by fear, not by a wish for justice or retribution.

Dragons and demons spring from this source, too, and it is not fanciful to see echoes of it even in the supposedly sophisticated twentieth century. Cancer, the Bomb, AIDS, global warming: there are plenty of candidates from which to choose your own dragon or demon.

It was this pagan strand more than any other that the early Church was smart enough to seize and turn to its advantage. It preached a greater power which would not only vanquish all other objects of fear but in a sense gather all their powers to itself, making it the most awe-ful source ever known. (A classic example is the story of St Walburga on page 68.) Put alongside this the political influence of the Church both in small communities and in the country as a whole and you begin to understand why so much of a village's life revolved around its church and its parson.

The more I learn about Dorset, the more I realise how much there is still to learn. This book has taught me a lot that I did not know. Mary Brown says in her Introduction that she has almost enough material to fill another book; I hope that we will not have to wait too long for it.

John Newth
Wareham
Dorset.

Sketch map of Dorset

INTRODUCTION

For me, the 'essence of Dorset' is a picture of a winding lane, high-banked and primrose studded, threading between lush, green meadows filled with calm cows. Overhead, a solitary lark trills on and on in a blue sky. Beyond the fields the softly rounded hills sweep away to the coast, their flanks cushioned with bluebell-deep woods and a soft undergrowth of fresh green bracken. I know exactly what Sir Frederick Treves meant when he said "the smell of cow manure is the incense of Dorset", for down that lane the smells are mingled, on a warm Spring day, with the animal warmth of cows.

When I decided to write this book I was eager to set down the many interesting stories I had gathered over a long period of study. Having many relations in Dorset and southern Somerset, I was fortunate to be able to draw on the memories of these 'elderly informers' to enrich the material I had gained elsewhere. In the cause of truth, over the last six months I have been (with husband Ken as photographer) to most of the places mentioned in this book. It has been a fascinating journey of discovery. We have scrambled down overgrown paths in search of secret chapels and holy wells — borne howling gales and driving rain in the interests of atmosphere, and driven around in circles looking for tiny, hidden churches.

Dorset is truly a county of contrasts — the bustle of the seaside towns and the crowded approaches to Poole and Bournemouth could not be further removed from the empty winding lanes around Batcombe and Hermitage, or the lonely clifftops near Bridport and Charmouth.

One problem was that so many illustrious writers have already 'done' Dorset, and it would be churlish to deny the enchantment with which I devoured Treves' *Highways and Byways of Dorset* some years back. Added to that was the delight of Darton and the evocative poetry of Barnes, while the comprehensive work on folklore by Udal brought many strands together. Hardy has been a long-standing favourite, as the one and only writer who can so clearly evoke the mood and character of a county. Hutchins was the first of a formidable group of historians contributing to the huge body of work on Dorset. All have been grist to the mill, though not without difficulty, as sources are often conflicting and one must take a middle course of circumspection.

Seeing the number of books already published on Dorset gave rise to the feeling that the task was impossible. It had all been done before. When I dug deeper I found that there were so many half-forgotten stories and remnants of old customs still remembered — that I would find it hard to keep the number of topics within a readable limit. At this stage I can only humbly present my contribution, conscious always of the debt I owe to the great writers of the past who have influenced my work, and more importantly fired me with the enthusiasm in the first place.

My only regret is for all the 'fragments' of the whole I have had to leave out for various reasons — the story of the 'Byzant' ceremony, for instance, a complicated mix of pagan rites and medieval practice, which ensured a water supply for the people of Shaftesbury; the unique game called 'Ringing the Bull' which is played in *The Three Choughs* in Blandford; the story of the mythical 'Wimborne donkey', a figment of the imagination of a local Lady of the Manor, who suspected a vicar of Papist practices! There are many more, almost enough to fill another book!

One of the things that intrigues me is the way that legends persist over hundreds of years, immortalised in folk memory, and still playing a part in the web of events and personalities that make up the present and the past of a county. Most of the sections which deal with country festivals cover a broad period from medieval times up to the early 1900s. It is very difficult to pinpoint exactly when an event began, or changed, or ended. Usually it is the case that medieval customs were grafted on to or replaced, earlier pagan ceremonies which had been 'Christianised' and later still adapted again to suit modern needs. It is often not possible to disentangle the different strands. Many old customs fell foul of the Reformation, when Henry VIII split with Rome — after which there was a great wave of anti-Catholic feeling for a period lasting well over 100 years. Church decorations were ripped out, even the Cross was seen as a decadent emblem. Anything which smacked of Catholic practice was stamped on — Guy Fawkes was pilloried more for his Papist beliefs than for the fact that he tried to blow up Parliament.

Churches figure a great deal in this book. This is not because I am particularly religious, but because in local churches, history is there for all to see. In carvings and symbols, local legends are often portrayed and important local figures are featured. Some of the smaller churches have a strong medieval ambience, such as the tiny church at Gussage St Andrew, sometimes called Minchington Church, where ancient wall-paintings tell the story of the Crucifixion. This shows how early, illiterate worshippers learned the elements of the Scriptures through brightly-coloured wall-paintings, which graphically depict, almost in strip-cartoon form, the Christian story.

Superstition and country lore are passed orally down the generations, unconsciously learned 'at Mother's knee'. While, like all things, they continually evolve and develop, there is evidence to suggest that the basic tenets expressed in this form change not at all; the grain of pagan origin can still be seen — clothed in modern garb. Where there is a strong oral tradition, many folklorists believe that this proves the truth of a legend far more convincingly than the written word ever could. It is an absorbing study and one which leads the seeker of knowledge into many other 'ologies'.

As for the legends and fairytales presented in this book, tales of hidden treasure, secret passages and miraculous happenings — I have to say ... I believe in all of them!

Mary Brown

This book is dedicated to my mother, Violet Baker of Edmondsham, Dorset.

CONTENTS

CONTENTS

Disappearing Bells

The eight bells destined for the old church at Poole were said to have been lost at sea near Old Harry Rocks, due to the 'impious behaviour' of the crew. Local tradition stated that on stormy nights when the waves were high the shipwrecked crew could be heard moaning, with the bells pealing from beneath the water.

So closely packed are the churches of England, that there are few places out of earshot of pealing bells, which down the centuries have called the people to prayer, warned them of danger, proclaimed victory in war and rung out joyously for community celebrations.

Bells have always been regarded with some awe and superstition, for many tales and legends exist in all parts of the country. A common theme is that of church bells being heard tolling underwater, where villages have been submerged, as in the 'Lost Land of Lyonnesse' off Cornwall. Some stories tell of peoples' lives being saved by recognising the church bells when lost and given up for dead. Dorset has a good share of bell legends and superstition, for instance at Longburton near Sherborne it was said that if the tenor bell sounded heavy and dull, someone in the parish would die within the week. There are also instances of the oil from church bells being used for healing purposes.

The most common bell stories in Dorset are of grand larceny, though it is hard to credit that such a large and heavy item as a church bell could be carried away, quite apart from the difficulties involved in disposing of it. At Bindon Abbey, after the Dissolution of the monasteries by Henry VIII, local feeling ran high, for the word got round that 'Fordington rogues' had stolen Bindon bells.

There are two different versions of the tale, the first being that when the monastery was closed down the twelve bells were to be divided between Combe Keynes and Wool, but the Fordington villagers carried off five of the twelve and hid them in 'Bell Drong', a narrow lane above the church. Later they came with wagons and took them away. The second version puts the robbery before the Dissolution, saying that while the Cistercian monks were actually at prayer, during Mass, the Fordington felons got into the tower, unshipped all twelve bells and loaded them silently into wagons! Unfortunately for them the twelfth one slipped and made a loud clang, whereupon the Abbot and monks gave chase, catching them about half a mile away. It seems that as a result of this confrontation, five bells were taken to Fordington and seven were returned, two of which went to Stinsford. However Hutchins says that Wool church had four of them, Combe Keynes had three and Fordington had five, one of the latter being melted down to make two, thus giving Fordington six. So the truth is unclear, especially as one historian also throws doubt on whether there ever were twelve bells, for the Cistercians specified austerity in all things, and officially the order allowed nothing more than a simple bell-cote with a single bell.

Knowlton Church, an eerie ruin beside the Wimborne to Cranborne road, also has a confused story of stolen bells. The site is said to be haunted and even now has a somewhat subdued atmosphere. The 12th century church probably replaced an earlier building which was built in the centre of a pagan earthwork, a Neolithic henge, perhaps a conscious attempt to 'Christianise' the site.

Two large bells at Shaftesbury Museum

Grand Larceny and the Devil's Work

The village is long since dead, possibly depopulated as a result of plague, and the church fell into disrepair about 1650. Hutchins reports that in 1550 Sir Richard Saunders was the curate, and that at that time there were three bells in the tower. In 'A Shepherd's Life' by W. H. Hudson, the shepherd Caleb Bawcombe at one time moved a few miles over the border with Wiltshire from his home village of Martin to work on a farm near Knowlton, calling it a 'land of strange things'. His version of the bell story was that the church became a ruin after the great bell was stolen by the Devil one stormy night. Later the villagers found that it had been flung into a small river a few miles away. Years later it could still be seen half-buried in the mud when the water level was low. But "all the King's horses and all the King's men" couldn't pull the bell up again, for the Devil was pulling the other way. Attempts were made to lift the bell, using a team of white oxen and strong ropes, but no sooner had they got the bell as far as the bank, than the ropes snapped and it fell back into the water. Caleb said it was still there, he had met a man who had seen it.

Yet another account, related in 1852, held that there had been a very valuable bell in Knowlton tower. Some robbers intended to steal it, take it to France and sell it. But they were pursued and overtaken on Sturminster Marshall bridge, so they threw it into the Stour and made off. Knowlton men let down ropes and nearly succeeded in raising the bell, but again the ropes broke and they were unsuccessful. The local saying was ...

"All the Devils in Hell
Could never pull up Knowlton bell."
also ... "Knowlton bell is stole,
And thrown into White Mill Hole."

It would seem that the disappearing bells of Dorset were always dear to the hearts of the people, for the dispossessed villagers of Milton Abbas stood at their doorways and wept when Lord Milton, having already swept away their old homes in the old town of Middleton to improve his view, had the old Abbey bells carted away in a fit of pique. Another stolen bell story comes from the village of Plush, near Dorchester.

William Barnes clearly shared the general feeling ..

"I seem to hear above my head,
The bell that in the tow'r was rung;
But whither went its iron tongue
That here bemoaned the long lost dead?"

The ruined church of Knowlton, near Cranborne

11

Shrove Tuesday Customs

Up to about a hundred years ago, Shrove Tuesday was a kind of 'Mardi-gras' of excess, rowdiness and cruelty. Everywhere in the country the day was an excuse for drunkenness and for the playing of wild games, seemingly in a 'last fling' before the austerities of the coming Lenten season.

As a Christian festival the day was important and for country folk it was one of the major holidays of the year, though not always 'holy' in the way it was originally intended.

First came 'Collop Monday' when any remaining meats were cut up into collops and eaten with eggs — then on Shrove Tuesday a holiday was declared while housewives rushed to use up all the rich spicy foods in their pantries in pancakes, before the 'Shriving-Bell' or 'Pancake-Bell' called everyone to church. The word 'Shrove' comes from 'shrive' meaning, to confess. The traditional food for the day was, and still is, the pancake, said to be lucky, for eating them on Shrove Tuesday ensured a year's good luck, with no shortage of food or money all year — but if eaten after 8 pm the luck would all be bad. The rest of the day after church was a holiday, given over to letting off steam in rough-and-tumble games and amusements.

There is considerable documentation about particular events in Dorset. William Barnes wrote at length on the subject, as did John Symonds Udal in his book, *Dorsetshire Folklore*.

The brutal sport of cock-fighting was one of the favourite sports up to the 19th century and every village had its 'cockpit' where the excited men gathered to place wagers on their fancied fighter. W. Chafin in 1816 in *Anecdotes Respecting Cranborne Chase* wrote that cock-fighting was a favourite diversion in the 18th century and that "cocks were bred for fighting at different lodges in the Chase". He goes on to say that "in our days of refinement, the amusement of cock-fighting hath been exploded and in a great measure abondoned, being deemed to be barbarous and cruel." Equally vicious was 'cock-squailing' which consisted of throwing sticks or other missiles at a cock tethered to a stake, which curious pastime was continued until the poor thing died. Tiny children were given cloth cocks to practice on. We know that these cruel games were played at Milton Abbas and at many other places throughout the county, as well as badger-baiting and bear-baiting.

Countrywide there was a tradition for rough football games on Shrove Tuesday, many of which survive to this day. The games were more like battles, often involving the whole village and usually entailing one side or the other finishing up in the stream! At Corfe Castle a special kind of football is still played by members of the Company of Marblers and Stone-cutters, who have a number of ancient ceremonies peculiar to themselves. The Shrove Tuesday game takes place along the road which led to Ower Quay, from whence the stone was shipped. The original purpose of the game was to maintain the right of way to the Quay. Presumably they always lost the ball, for on the next day, Ash Wednesday, the proprietors of the Quay, under some old agreement, paid to the stone company one pound of pepper and a new football. Which was, as Treves comments, 'a strange commercial instrument' — but at least it gave the men a ball to play with next year.

The most well-known Shrove Tuesday custom

Crazy Games, Cruel Sports and Lent-crocking

in Dorset was 'Lent-crocking', carried on at Piddlehinton and Sherborne until the end of the last century. There are also reports of its late survival at Marnhull, Blandford, Portland, Lulworth and Stalbridge, while at Durweston a Mr Valentine Richmond who died in 1925 left a bequest specifically to ensure that the custom was kept alive.

Parties of children would go round the village, 'a-shroving', knocking at front doors and asking for pancakes or bread and cheese. If refused they would then bombard the door with broken crocks or shards. J. S. Udal quotes the rhyme the mischievous children sang while enjoying this naughty game ...

"I'm come a-shroving,
For a piece of pancake,
Or a piece of bacon,
Or a little truckle cheese
Of your own making.
Give me some, or give me none,
Or else your door shall have a stone."

A report in 1889 stated that an enterprising schoolmaster at Cerne got the children to throw logs instead of crocks, thereby building up his fuel supply! In later years the custom was gradually discontinued, and two Dorset women were actually taken to court for damaging a door. William Barnes suggested that the significance of the broken crocks indicated that the pots were not needed for cooking during Lent.

After the fun and frolics came the solemnities of Ash Wednesday. In pre-Reformation times, penitents went to church to have their foreheads marked with a cross of ashes. This solemn day marked the beginning of Lent, and meant six weeks of austerity before the joyous Christian festival of Easter arrived. Sweetmeats and rich Easter eggs brought an end to the fast, corresponding with the return of Spring after the long, cold winter.

The cruel sport of 'cock-squailing'

Bear-baiting, popular since medieval times

13

Village Names and Nicknames

Any fellow from Winterbourne Houghton out after dark was likely to be jeered and whistled at and called a 'Houghton owl', though whether those who whistled really knew how the epithet came to be used is hard to say. The story goes that one John Joyce once got lost in the woods and called our fearfully, "Man lost — man lost!" He was answered only by a hooting owl, and was so simple-minded that he took it for a human voice. The story is re-told by Hardy, in *Far From The Madding Crowd*, when Joseph Poorgrass is frightened at being out in the dark.

The application of nicknames to inhabitants of certain villages is common in any county and Dorset is not lacking in this respect. Ansty men were called 'Ansty Shear-dogs', for Ansty was famous both for its gang of sheep-shearers and its beer. The tale was told that once an Ansty sheep-shearer got so drunk on the local brew that he tried to shear a sheepdog! Mappowder men were called 'Hedge-pigs', for two Mappowder men were once mistaken for gypsies, Mappowder being a known meeting-place for the wandering tribes. Gypsies' fondness for the delicate taste of roast hedgehog led to this epithet. Hazelbury Bryan lads were known as 'Baa-lambs' for they too were sheep-men. Unfortunately a few of them gave the village a bad name for sheep-stealing. Other 'animal' names include 'Buckland Nanny-goats', also 'Sturminster Newton Nanny-goats', and 'Pulham Hogs', though the reasons for these are not clear. Wareham people were called 'Cuckoos' on account of a far-fetched tale about a man who tried to fence in a cuckoo at the end of the season to prevent him flying away — it was believed that the late arrival of the cuckoo next

Spring would make the harvest late.

There was much rivalry at one time in cudgel-playing and cut-leg, between the villages of Holwell and Caundle, so they were called, respectively, 'Holwell Men' and 'Caundle Dogs'. The fellows from Fifehead were known as 'Bulldogs', for prowess in what field we do not know. The women who worked in the fields around Batcombe at hay-making time were known as 'Batcombe Boys', again the reason is somewhat obscure.

Dorset place-names offer an interesting mix of Roman, Saxon and Norman roots which have developed over the centuries. For instance, 'Stauro' is Latin for a 'strong river', while 'Minster' reveals the existence of an early religious centre; 'Newton' is literally 'new town' — and the whole becomes 'Sturminster Newton', really two towns, one on each side of the river. Shillingstone began as 'Schellings-ton' for the land here belonged to a Norman family, the Eschellings. 'Tun' always meant town or village, 'Bury' is the equivalent of 'burgh', meaning a fortified house, manor or town. 'Bourne' a river, and any village name ending in 'Abbas' signified that the village was the property of the Abbey, such as Melbury Abbas and Bradford Abbas.

Whole strings of villages in Dorset have the same first name, like the Winterbornes, of which there are fourteen, though often, as at Came, only the second name is commonly used. The Winterbornes get their name from a natural phenomenon; a stream which dries up in the summer — and runs again only when the winter rains arrive. According to H. J. Moule, the actual moment of a winter-borne breaking has never

Owls, Cuckoos and Baa-lambs

been seen by Man, and he quotes the story of a two-week vigil being kept by a man at Winterborne Abbas, who turned his back for only a few minutes and missed the crucial moment! Another group of villages are the Tarrants, of which there are eight, named after the River Tarrant. There are also the Gussages, three in number. The 'Piddles' and 'Puddles' all get their name from the River Piddle, and it is interesting to consider the evolution of the name of Piddletrenthide. In the Domesday Book, the area was assessed at 30 hides and was therefore called 'Pidele Trentehydes', 'trente' being old French for thirty. By 1314 the name had become 'Pudele Thrittyhide', keeping the element referring to its acreage. The present name is nearer, as one can see, to the original.

An old legend links the three villages of Child Okeford, Shillingstone, and Okeford Fitzpaine (Fitzpaine means fivepenny). The legend tells how an abandoned child was found in the church porch at Shillingstone and the three villages decided what was to be done. Shillingstone gave one shilling to support the child, Fitzpaine gave fivepence and the village of Child Okeford actually raised the child. One version of the legend says that Christ (the Child) was seen in Child Okeford, and that the other two villages gave him the different sums of money.

Farm and field names often graphically describe the type of land, such as 'Starvington Farm', 'Poor Lot' and 'Hungry Down', which reflect the poor quality of the land, as does 'Labour-in Vain' Farm. Any field name having 'gara', or more usually 'gore' meant a triangular piece of land; often fields were known by a name which showed that the rent from them was used for charity, such as 'Charity Bottom' and 'Lamp Ground Mead' at Powerstock, where the rent from this piece of ground was used to maintain the sanctuary lamp in the church. The field name 'Butts' indicated that there was once an archery practice held there at a time when even small villages had to provide a bowman or two for the King's army. Village names too, show this attachment to place — such as Toller Porcorum, meaning 'Toller of the pigs', sometimes called 'Swine's Toller' or 'Hog's Toller', for this was a favoured place for grazing pigs. Toller Fratrum was 'Toller of the Brethren', for here was a house of the Order of St John of Jerusalem.

This is a rich field which certainly repays study and gives more insight than one might at first suppose into the secrets of old Dorset.

A sheep-shearing gang in 1885

15

Crime and Punishment

"On August 25th 1631, Jo Kay and Nicholas Sims did play at All Saints in sermon time, and laughed, and Sims did stick Kay a box on the ear and carry themselves very unreverently."

Both Kay and Sims were sent to prison for this offence, which occurred in Dorchester — for at that time improper behaviour in Church or on the Sabbath was regarded very severely. People were fined for absence from church or for leaving the service early.

Another crime of the day warranting severe punishment was drunkenness, as in the case of Robert Foot, who in 1632 was charged with being "severall tymes drunke and wishing that fire and brimstone would fall on this town, it being sufficiently proud." He too was sent to prison and "sett close to worke" for his sins. Around the same time, women who 'scolded' were punished, by being 'plounced' or ducked, though to be fair, the magistrates at Dorchester did wait for the weather to warm up before ducking one Mary Tuxberry. Other culprits were placed in the stocks which were to be found on every village green.

Perhaps the most degrading of all punishments were the instances of 'Church Penance', often exacted for adultery. One such case was that of Susannah Philips at Bishop's Caundle, who in 1785 was made to stand throughout the service draped in a white linen sheet, reciting confessional phrases. Her 'crime' was that she had given birth to an illegitimate or 'base-born' child.

From early times civil offences such as selling short measures of ale, were punished by fines, as were transgressions against wood-gathering rights.

Sheep-stealing was much more serious and was punishable by death up to 1827. Considering the extreme poverty of farm labourers in the early 19th Century it is hardly surprising that many offences of this kind occurred. A story from East Stour tells how several poor families conspired to steal a sheep at night. The sheep was to be quickly butchered and shared out. The men who carried out a door-to-door search in pursuit of the offenders saw nothing unusual when they called at one house where a woman, sitting on what appeared to be a low stool was nursing her baby. She arose rather quickly when they left, for she had been sitting on a hot stew-pot full of succulent mutton. She had hastily removed it from the fire when the men knocked. Her husband escaped punishment, while his accomplices were jailed for 18 months.

Poaching was the cause of constant battles between some country folk and the Chase keepers. Many bloody battles were fought between gangs of poachers and the Lord's men, employed to keep the game preserves intact. There are reports of venison being hidden in Pimperne Church tower and in an empty tomb at Sixpenny Handley. As early as the 14th century poaching was recorded on the lands of Forde Abbey when two men were charged with taking £5 worth of fish and hares and rabbits from the Abbot's warren. It is not in the least surprising to us today, that poor people resented the fact that wild game and rabbits were only the preserve of the rich. In times of poverty and near-starvation they naturally took from 'nature's table' what they needed to feed their families.

Dorset was no more or less law-abiding than

The ducking-stool, used for 'scolds'

Unrest and Uprisings in Dorset

any other county, but there were certainly several very important cases of what might be called 'crimes against the state', which we would now call 'popular uprising'. The first of these was the rising of the 'Clubmen' during the Civil War. They were a body of some 5000 men from Somerset, Dorset, Wiltshire and Hampshire. Ordinary farming folk who had had enough of their crops being destroyed and their farms vandalised, as the Parliamentary and Royalist forces pursued their battles across the face of the southern counties.

They made a banner which read …

"If you offer to plunder or take our cattle,
Be assured we will give you battle".

This fine body of men lasted through several skirmishes with Cromwell's New Model army, until in August 1645 a large company were overcome and captured on Hambledon Hill. Cromwell wrote to his commander …

"They are poor silly creatures, whom if you please to let me send them home, they promise to be very dutiful for time to come and will be hanged before they come out again."

So the 'poor silly creatures' went home, relieved that they had escaped without punishment, and this remarkable protest ended not with a bang but a whimper.

The hideous atrocities of the Bloody Assize are well-known and stories about how blood dripped from the hacked-off quarters of those who supported Monmouth, as they hung from the tall church towers of Dorset, have been told many times. In Dorchester nearly 350 men appeared before Jeffreys. Seventy-four were hanged and one hundred and seventy-five

transported for life, leaving from Weymouth in three ships bound for Barbados.

In 1830 the 'Captain Swing' riots began, involving farm-workers from Wiltshire and Dorset. There was arson, the breaking of the hated threshing machines which had made many men redundant, and a widespread demand for decent wages. In Dorset there were 42 incidents, 12 fires and 10 cases of agricultural machines being smashed. Very harsh sentences were imposed. Of the men tried in the county; thirty-three were acquitted, one was whipped, fifteen were jailed, thirteen were transported and six were sentenced to die.

These events led directly to the attempt by the six men of Tolpuddle to form a Union and so to ensure fair wages and just treatment for the working man. The treatment they received for their pains was most unjust — and the Tolpuddle Martyrs are not forgotten by present-day Trade Unionists who hold a rally in Tolpuddle every summer.

The stocks, once a familiar sight in every village. Wimborne St. Giles

St Catherine's Chapels

Up to about a hundred years ago, St Catherine of Alexandria was the favourite saint of unmarried women, who would invoke her aid in finding a husband. For St Catherine was named as the patron saint of spinsters, and also of hilltops — in a strange juxtaposition of beliefs which has been bequeathed to us from the past.

The age-old Christian legend tells how St. Catherine, having been abducted by the Romans in the year 307 AD, refused to renounce her Christian faith. She also refused to marry the Emperor, which gave rise to her other name, 'the bride of Christ' — she held her own against fifty philosophers who tried to shake her knowledge of the Christian faith. The stand she took enraged her captors, who tried to murder her in a most horrific fashion, bound to a wheel set with sharp knives (hence — the Catherine Wheel). But the wheel broke and her devout followers naturally said this was caused by divine intervention. Her tormentors were thus forced to kill her by beheading, a much quicker death.

She came to be known as the patron saint of unmarried girls because of her refusal to marry; of the clergy and students because of her learning; of nurses because it was said that milk, not blood, flowed from her severed head; and of all those whose work was concerned with the wheel, such as wheelrights, millers and spinners. Sixty-two churches are dedicated to her in this country alone, and she is shown in many religious paintings and stained glass windows, always accompanied by the wheel.

After her death, legend tells that her body was carried to Mount Sinai by angels, and it is because of this connection that St Catherine became associated with hilltops. All over the country there are St Catherine's Hills, topped by small chapels dedicated to her. Several of these are in Dorset, the most famous being the sturdy, stone construction of Abbotsbury, high on the hill above that picturesque village. This stout building can be seen for many miles around, and for centuries was a landmark for sailors along the treacherous Dorset coast. At times a man with a horn would sit up there on the lookout for shoals of fish, blowing the horn to alert the fishermen when one appeared.

The massively constructed chapel measures 45 feet by 15 feet, with enormous buttresses to hold up the barrel-vaulted roof. There is no timber at all in the construction, even the roof and ceiling are of stone. The chapel was built sometime around the beginning of the 15th century as a chantry for sailors and as a sea-mark and lookout post. The most extraordinary facet of the memories contained in these massive stones is the ancient custom of making votive offerings to St Catherine, by young girls who sought her aid in finding a husband. They would drop pins into a cavity, place their hands and one knee into the 'wishing holes' which can still be seen in the south doorway, and then recite a prayer or charm to obtain their heart's desire ....

"A husband, St. Catherine,
A handsome one, St. Catherine,
A rich one, St. Catherine,
A nice one, St. Catherine,
And soon, St. Catherine!"

St. Catherine's Chapel at Milton Abbas stands at the top of a long flight of turf steps leading up from the Abbey grounds to its hidden location

The tiny chapel in the woods at Milton Abbas

in the woods. King Athelstan spent the night of July 28th, St Sampson's Day, on this spot on his way north to a battle. Here, it is said, he had a vision of victory, and was so moved and overjoyed that he founded the great Abbey, dedicating it to St Sampson among others, and bestowing great treasures and property upon the foundation. When Milton Abbey was pulled down after the dissolution, some of the stone was used to build a gothic West front for the little chapel. Later the tiny sanctuary fell upon hard times, for it became a pigeon house and later still a labourer's cottage — although now its status as a chapel has been restored. Milton Abbey also owned property at Holworth, scene of the 'Burning Cliff' incident described elsewhere in this book. Here too a tiny St. Catherine's Chapel was built on top of the cliffs.

At Cerne, to the North-East of the town, on 'Cat-and-Chapel Hill' (a corruption of Catherine-and-Chapel) there was once a ruined chapel belonging to the Abbey of Cerne. No trace of it now remains, nor is Cat-and-Chapel Hill mentioned on modern maps, but it lies to the side of the steep road to Piddletrenthide.

An interesting footnote to this story is that it was reported in *Purbeck Papers* that young girls in the mid-18th century also said charms to obtain a husband, at St. Aldhelm's Chapel, down the coast at St. Aldhelm's Head, near Swanage — perhaps in the mistaken belief that this chapel too, being on a hilltop, was also dedicated to St. Catherine. They used the same form of invocation and offered pins to make their wishes come true.

This type of legend, having roots at least 1500 years old, and having its elements passed down through many generations, offers an interesting insight into how religious beliefs become confused with superstition to produce a charming nugget of local lore.

St. Catherine, always shown with her wheel

St. Catherine's Chapel, Abbotsbury

Dreadful Visitations

"... then the fire roared dreadfully; the lead melted, the stones split and flew; so fervent and irresistible was the heat, that the bells dissolved and ran down in streams ..."

This was the alarming report of the Great Fire of Blandford in 1731. The town had, in fact, plenty of experience of fires, but this one was by far the worst. The town was nearly destroyed in 1579 and it was then considered necessary to impose a fine on people whose chimneys caught fire in the town. This measure did not prevent further outbreaks, for there were later fires in 1677 and 1713. The devastating fire of 1731 began at about 2 pm on a June afternoon, at a tallow-chandler's house. The fire took hold quickly and raged until all but forty houses were destroyed. Both the church and Town Hall were gone and the fire even spread to the villages of Bryanston and Blandford St. Mary. At the time there was an epidemic of smallpox raging in the town, which led to pathetic scenes as sick people were carried out and laid in safe places — but at least the fire wiped out the disease. Modern Blandford has few buildings of an earlier date than 1731 and now appears a robust, Georgian town. The Bastard brothers rebuilt the town in noble style and the classic pump by the Church was put up in remembrance of "God's dreadful visitation by Fire".

'Sweet Be'mi'ster' too, was prone to incendiary accidents. It is a charming market town dominated by the glorious 16th Century church tower, with its many pinnacles and ornaments, on which were once incongruously hung the bloody quarters of some of Monmouth's followers. Like Blandford the town has few really old buildings. The worst fire took place during the Civil War, and was caused by ...

"a musket discharged in the gable, and was wild fire, and the winde directly with the towne; so the whole towne was destroyed in two hours."

Luckily, the lovely church tower escaped, and did so again in the later fires of 1684 and 1781.

The picture of Dorchester's history too, is scorched by the ravages of fire. There were outbreaks in 1613, 1622, 1725 and 1775. The worst was in 1613, which, like the fire at Blandford, began in a tallow-chandler's house. The month was August and many were away in the fields helping with the harvest, returning to find their homes a pile of smouldering ruins. Three hundred houses were destroyed and two of the three churches in the town were lost, leaving only St Peter's. After this dreadful day, strong measures were taken, so that the later fires were indeed less damaging. Precautions included the ordering of leather buckets to hang in the church in 1640. In June 1649 between £30 and £40 was paid for a "Brazen engine or spoute to quench fire in times of danger". This was a brass pump held by two men and worked by a third. By 1653 each parish had two officials appointed to inspect for "bad or dangerous chymnyes or mantells, and to see that all persons keep their wells, buckets, ropes, tanckets, malkins and ladders fit to make use of upon occasion."

Poor little Wareham was the worst hit. Treves, as always, shows much sympathy ....

"It's history is one long lurid account of

Old Wareham, about 1910

Dorset Towns Consumed by Fire

disaster and woe, so that it would need a Jeremiah to tell all its lamentations. Possibly no town in England has been besieged so often and so readily, or has been so many times burnt and reduced to ruins. ... It is famous for little but its calamities ... It would almost seem as if the habit of being burnt became established in the settlement, for in 1762, after a hundred years of peace, Wareham set fire to itself with such effect that nearly the whole of its houses were reduced to ashes."

The fire had started one Sunday in July when hot ashes had been carelessly thrown out. The wind helped the fire by changing direction and the summer-dry thatched roofs quickly caught, one after another. In four hours one hundred and thirty houses were destroyed. The churches and the Town Hall somehow escaped the blaze and the Dorset historian Hutchins, who was away from home, returned to find his house gone, and little saved except a few sticks of furniture. His poor wife had a narrow escape, being surrounded by burning buildings, and none of the great man's sermons or books was saved, although the notes for his famous *History* were not destroyed.

The strangest Dorset fire was the phenomenon known as 'The Burning Cliff' which took place on Holworth Cliff above Ringstead Bay. The land here once belonged to the monks of Milton Abbey, who obtained their salt and fish from here. In 1827 a remarkable 'local volcano' appeared quite suddenly, caused, it is said, by spontaneous combustion of bituminous shale. There were 'voluminous' flames and 'exhalations of sulphurous vapour'. A strange sight indeed for

the Dorset coast. The cliff, still known as 'Burning Cliff' continued to smoulder for some time, and drew large numbers of visitors to the area who came to marvel at the sight. One commentator says that the origin of the fire was attributed to the decomposition of iron pyrites in the strata and that the activity became more vigorous at the time of the spring tides.

This area must have become quite used to 'gaping tourists', for in March 1815 an area of the cliff, two acres in extent, and including a cottage with a garden, slid down 30 feet or more. Within three years the cottage had travelled 500 feet towards the sea, garden still intact, but 200 feet lower than its original position. Twelve years after its first slip the cottage finally fell into the sea.

A similar outbreak of fire occurred on the 'Burning Mountain', on the cliffs between Lyme Regis and Charmouth. It ignited first in 1751 and then again in the early years of this century.

Sixpenny Handley after a fire in 1892, when 186 people were made homeless

Superstition, Divination and Charms

Dancing barefoot over furze twigs on the floor was the fate of an elder daughter who remained unmarried on her younger sister's wedding day, according to *Notes and Queries* at the end of the last century.

No wonder that love divination was so keenly practised by the young ladies of the time, who not only needed to know who their future husband might be, but also when they would be wed. Country girls made balls of cowslip flowers called 'tosty-balls' and played a game of tossing them to each other in a circle, calling out the names of certain young men as they did so. If the ball was dropped then the last-mentioned young man would be the happy bridegroom-to-be, and the girl who dropped it would be the bride. Various other charms were used for similar purposes, such as scattering hemp seed in the churchyard at midnight on Midsummer Eve, or placing nuts on the bars of the fire at Hallowe'en — either of these would hopefully produce an apparition of the lucky man. Asking the cuckoo, "How many years till I be wed?" would result in the cuckoo giving a certain number of calls in answer to the question.

Old people would ask the cuckoo how many years it would be until they died. It was also said that the reason why the cuckoo never built its own nest was that it was too busy answering questions! The strange habits of the elusive cuckoo led to many superstitious beliefs about the bird, for some said that cuckoos do not migrate in winter, but that they turn into hawks instead. Another theory was that they somehow became fairy hills. Also whatever a person is doing when he first hears the cuckoo, that is (more or less) what he will be doing for the next twelve months. If his pockets are full of money at the time, then he will never want for anything in the next year.

Most birds were thought to have mystical connections and a bird tapping on the window was thought to be an omen of death. A cock crowing in the daytime was also a feared portent and if a raven croaked while flying over a person, that person would surely die before long. It was believed to be very unlucky to kill a robin and anyone who did so would find that their little finger had grown crooked. An owl's heart carried into battle was a good luck charm and would protect the bearer from injury or death, but if the owl's heart was placed on the left breast of a sleeping woman, she would tell all her secrets! Magpies had strong connections with the Devil, and the well-known rhyme tells what to expect if you see several of the birds together ...

"One for sorrow, two for joy,
Three for a girl, four for a boy,
Five for silver, six for gold,
Seven for a secret never to be told ..."

Country children to this day, know that if you see just one magpie, you should wave at it to ward off the attendant bad luck.

Other creatures too, had superstitions attached to them, for instance, the number of spots on ladybirds was said to foretell the price of wheat, in shillings per bushel. A toad going over one's foot was especially unlucky, for toads were thought to be witches' 'familiars'. Hares too, were regarded with fear, for the same reason, indeed a hare was often thought to be a witch in disguise, and she could only be killed in certain magical ways, (see Chapter 31). Udal quotes several

One for Sorrow, Two for Joy ...

instances of such stories from the Isle of Purbeck in the 1890s.

Flower-lore is rich in superstition and it was widely thought to be unlucky to bring certain flowers into the house, especially the hawthorn or may, snowdrops, and according to this dialect rhyme, (quoted in *Dorset County Chronicle* at the end of the 19th century) furze bloom as well ...

"If the yaller vuz be a-card in,
A-thin a year there's nar a doubt —
A coffin'll be a-card out."

In every part of the country there were numerous superstitions about death. If a mattress was stuffed with pigeon feathers a person could not die 'easily'. Also the bed should be placed parallel to the floorboards, though some believed that it would be easier if the dying person were lifted out of bed and placed on the floor itself! Doors and windows were opened to make the soul's departure easier. If the corpse did not stiffen after death, it was said that another death would soon follow. Mourners should never run after a funeral, nor walk three abreast. In Lulworth there was a report of bodies being buried with a penny in one hand and a hammer in the other. Of a similarly obscure nature was the pagan custom of placing a bowl of salt on the chest of the cadaver as a charm against evil spirits.

Babies and birth too, needed protection, not so long ago it was believed that a child should be carried up to the top of the house before being taken downstairs for the first time. Also that if a pregnant woman is frightened by something, she should remember to clap her hand to her body, not to her face, or the baby's face would be marked. Cats were to be kept away from the cot,

for they would 'steal the baby's breath' if they got in.

As everywhere in this weather-obsessed country, weather superstitions are the most numerous of all, and a great many are still current today. A specifically Dorset saying states that if Hardy's monument can be seen from Dorchester it is a sure sign of bad weather. It was said that if the sun shone through the branches of the apple trees on Old Christmas Day, it is a sign of a good 'blooth', or blossoming, bringing prosperity. Also that 'a green Christmas makes a fat churchyard'.

But from the *Dorset County Chronicle* in 1891, comes the most wide-ranging and doom-laden prophecy of all ...

"If New Year's day be on a Thursday ... winter and summer windie.
A rainie harvest. Therefore we shall have over-flowings. Much fruit. Plentie of honey. Yet flesh shall be deare: cattle in general shall die: great troubles: warres:"

"Which nut will pop first?" Anxious girls on Hallowe'en

Dorset Fairs

'Gentry Day' at the Fair

Where, 200 years ago, could a country lad pay a penny to see a giant, see jugglers and conjurors, buy ribbons and tawdry jewellery for his lady-love, have his fortune told, and get gloriously drunk on furmity, all in one day? At one of Dorset's great fairs, that's where.

Fairs, like markets were granted by Charter, often to the Church and often held on the Feast Day of the saint to which the church was dedicated, as at Milton Abbas, where St Sampson's Fair was held on St Sampson's Eve and Day, the 27th and 28th of July. Fairs gave ordinary people a chance to see new sights, meet people, and to enjoy a few hours respite from the hard grind of working life. Some fairs lasted several days, and many towns had several fairs each year. With the grant of a fair came the right to close local shops and to collect tolls from the stallholders. The largest fairs in neighbouring counties were Weyhill, near Andover where Hardy's Michael Henchard got drunk and sold his wife, Susan, and the huge Whitedown Fair near Chard which was held in Whit week. Many Dorset folk made the effort to go such distances, for traders came from far and near, including weavers, bakers, saddlers, drapers, pedlars, cattlemen and horse dealers, shoe makers, cutlers — every trade was represented — as well as the tricksters, thieves and hucksters who sold faulty goods before quickly disappearing.

Autumn fairs were often 'Hiring Fairs' where shepherds would stand with their crooks, carters with their whips, as an advertisement, as it were, for potential employers, taking on new staff at Michaelmas. Around them was a hectic scene, as people streamed in from all directions, dealers with their laden carts, pack-men with their bundles and drovers with their sheep and cattle, all heading for the Fair.

Almost every Dorset town had its own Fair. Yetminster had a three-day event; Sturminster Newton Fair dated from medieval times and reportedly had rows of stalls in the square, plus such perennial attractions as a fat lady and a dwarf. Shaftesbury's 'Fair of St. Edward' lasted four days, while the Abbot of Forde was granted a six-day fair by Edward III which began on Easter Tuesday. Shroton Fair was of some importance at one time, and at Toller Down the fair was held on a hilltop from the reign of Charles II, while at Portesham, 'Possum Fes' Week began on August 6th and lasted all week. Seatown had a Fair on Whit Monday said to be 'sacred to the eating of Furmity', where the said delight was sold for a penny a plateful.

Woodbury Hill Fair was probably the most famous Fair in Dorset. It was granted by Charter in the time of Henry III and formerly lasted for five days, beginning on the 18th of September, near the feast of the Nativity of the Virgin Mary. The first day was 'Wholesale Day', the second day was 'Gentlefolks Day', with amusements and refreshments which included oysters and roast pork. Day three was 'All Folk's Day', and day four was 'Sheep Fair Day'. On the last day it was 'Pack-a-Penny Day', when all unsold goods were disposed of cheaply. Local legend says that this huge fair, which drew folk from all over the south of England, began when a single 'chapman' got caught in a storm and laid his goods out on the side of the hill to get them dry.

Pack Monday Fair at Sherborne was also a great attraction, and has remained so right up to

Conjurors, acrobats and all the fun of the fair

the present day. It is held on the first Monday after Old Michaelmas day in October. The local story is that on this day in 1490 the great abbey was finally completed and the masons and workmen packed up their tools to leave — hence 'Pack Monday'. In former times the Fair was chiefly for sheep, cattle and horses, but when this business was over, the thirst for enjoyment of the local people took over. The range of items for sale was enormous, cloth, earthenware, onions, walnuts, hazelnuts, apple and other fruit trees, toys, gingerbread, sweetmeats, sugar-plums, drapery, hats, boots, leather goods, bonnets, ribbons and lace.

The strange thing about Pack Monday Fair was that it began in the middle of the night with bands of local young men and boys roaming the streets from midnight on, kicking up an "incessant din the whole time with horns, bugles, and all sorts of tin trays that would make a noise . . ." This band of ruffians was known as 'Teddy Roe's Band', and they were still performing this cacophanous duty well into the 1940s.

An interesting feature of these fairs is that at one time there were in each town, what we would call 'Kangaroo Courts' for dealing with offences committed at fairs. These were called 'Courts of Pie Powder'. *Hone's Everyday Book*, (1825) says they were ... "the lowest and most expeditious court of justice known to the law of England. This court of record, incident to every fair and market, exists to administer justice for all commercial injuries concerned with the fair or market, the steward of him who owns the toll is the judge. The injury therefore, must be done, complained of, and redressed, within the compass of one and the same day, unless the fair continues longer". The curious title 'Pie Powder' is said to derive from 'pie-poudre' from the dusty feet of the suitors — or because justice is done as speedily as dust can fall from the feet. Hone however inclines to the view that it derives from 'pied puldreaux' (a 'pedlar' in Old French) signifying the court of pedlars and chapmen.

As we have seen Dorset folk never needed much encouragement to find an excuse for fun and games. Whenever the gibbet was erected for a hanging in Dorchester, a 'Hang Fair' was quickly organised near the grisly spectacle, so that bystanders could get refreshments during the proceedings and perhaps amuse themselves while awaiting the main event of the day.

Fish-seller at Burton Bradstock, about 1885

Mother Tongue

William Barnes, the Dorset dialect poet

When I first took my London-born husband to see my elderly aunt who lives near Sherborne, he couldn't understand a word she said! Hers is an accent of the borderland between Somerset and Dorset, and there is little to choose between the two at this point. When I read the poems of that great dialect poet William Barnes, I am instantly reminded of my grandfather, who was a countryman born and bred. The pronunciation of such words as ceake and meake (for 'cake' and 'make') as Barnes used them are as exact a rendition as one could get to the actual vowel sounds used.

'Thic' for 'that' is often quoted as being a typical Dorset word, and it was used in Somerset also to indicate 'that dog' or 'that object'. Likewise 'gurt' for 'great' or 'large' is common to both counties. Certain patterns of speech also sound familiar in my mind. Instead of 'Look!' grandfather would say 'Look zee!' 'Cassn't' and 'dussn't' served for 'can't' and 'don't', and 'bide still', instead of 'stay still'. A cute child or a small dog was 'a mommet', while anger was expressed succinctly as 'do make I wild'. 'Worse' was 'wuss' and 'curse' was 'cuss'. To be smart enough not to get caught by someone was to 'be upzides wi'en', for the character in question was probably a 'fly one'. A naughty or whining child was a 'proper wagwant', and a favourite exclamation of surprise or disgust was "S'hup me John", meaning, as I was told at a very early age, "So help me, John".

As country children we spent many happy hours wandering the lanes and woods, arms filled with summer flowers, or in autumn with pockets bulging full of nuts or mushrooms. Wild flowers had their own local names. 'Granfy greagle' was the wild orchid, very common 40 years ago in the fields and meadows, along with acres of nodding cowslips. The lanes were filled with 'Lady's Lace', which was our generic name for all the umbelliferous white-flowered plants which line the summer verges. The tall waving 'mowing-grass' of the hay meadows was filled with poppies and tall ox-eye daisies, which we knew as 'thunder-daisies'.

Wild creatures too, had their own names. Ants were 'emmets' and gnats were 'midges'. The huge May-bug which sometimes got into the house and flung itself against the window while we cowered under the bedclothes, was called a 'dummadore'. Frogs were always 'hog-frogs' and a wasp was always either a 'wops' or a 'waasp' with a long 'a' sound as in 'grasp'. A horse was always a 'hoss' and the velvety black mole was a 'want'.

At least as vividly remembered as the actual dialect words are the figures of speech used by all the adult members of the family. Cliches all, but full of homespun truth and readily understood by all in the immediate circle. A person who could not be trusted was 'as artful as a wagon-load of monkeys', a 'scamp', or a 'scallywag'. A woman with 'a past' was 'No better than she ought to be'. An odd person like the proverbial 'village idiot' was a 'dafty'. If a person looked sad, someone would be sure to say, 'You look as if you've lost a shilling and found sixpence'! A very slow person was 'too slow for a first-class funeral', while a person late for work was 'all behind like the cow's tail'. A short-lived pleasure was 'short and sweet, like a donkey's gallop', while a disappointment or disaster was tersely expressed by Father as a 'bad job', with all hopes 'Gone West'. A childless

Survival of an Ancient Language

woman had 'neet chick ner chiel'. Tea was 'the cup that cheers', and the talkative neighbour who arrived to share it 'could talk the hind leg off a donkey'.

As William Barnes walked the Dorset lanes last century, his keen ear was able to pick up not only the nuances of pronunciation and the actual dialect words, but also a sense of what made the people 'tick', so that his subjects were usually homely descriptions of local and sometimes mundane events, giving a feeling of truth and accuracy in every poem, as well as a sense of the essential simplicity and serenity of the country life. Perhaps this poem, 'The Shepherd o' the Farm', best shows the simple delights he is so good at conveying ...

"An' I do go to washèn pool,
A-sousèn over head an' ears
The shaggy sheep, to cleän their wool
An' meäke 'em ready for the shears.

An' when the shearèn time do come
Then we do work vrom dawn till dark;
Where zome do shear the sheep, and zome
Do mark their zides wi' meäster's mark.

An' when the shearèn's all a-done
Then we do eat, an' drink, an' zing
In meäster's kitchen till the tun
Wi' merry sounds do sheake and ring.

Oh! I be shepherd o' the farm,
Wi' tinklèn bells and sheep-dog's bark,
An' wi' my crook a-thirt my eärm
Here I do rove below the lark."

Barnes was a philologist as well as a poet and he believed that the Dorset dialect was directly descended from the old Saxon tongue; and should not be seen as a corruption of language, but rather as an older form of language. Naturally, since the development of the Education system in the late 19th Century and the increased mobility enjoyed by sophisticated country folk of today, true dialect speakers are now few and far between.

The author's grandfather, Charl Holt, working on the roads near the Somerset/Dorset border.

"Harvest Home!"

"... Crown'd with the eares of corne, now come,
And, to the pipe, sing Harvest Home.
Come forth, my Lord, and see the cart
Drest up with all the Country Art.

Robert Herrick's poem gives a charming picture of the happy country scene which followed a successful harvest.

In a rural population dependent on the moods of Mother Nature, a successful harvest is a natural object of joyous celebration. The farmer's prosperity was dependent on the produce of his land and a full barn meant food and income for the following year. All over the British Isles, farmers, their labourers and their families worked round the clock while the weather held, to get the harvest in. As the last high-piled wagon or 'Hock-Cart' lumbered into the rickyard, the cheer would go up ..."Harvest-home, harvest-home!" — the young people wearing straw crowns, dancing round the cart, full of eager anticipation for the great 'Harvest Supper' which would soon follow. Again Robert Herrick describes the scene for us ...

"Well on, brave boyes, to your Lord's Hearth,
Glitt'ring with fire; where, for your mirth,
Ye shall see first the large and cheefe
Foundation of your feast, fat Beefe:
With upper stories, Mutton, Veale
And Bacon ....
As here a custard, there a Pie,
And here all tempting Frumentie,

And for to make the merry cheere,

Those with a shout, and these with laughter.
Some blesse the cart, some kisse the sheaves;
Some prank them up with oaken leaves:"

If smirking wine be wanting here,
There's that, which drowns all care, stout Beere;
Which freely drink to your Lord's health,
Then to the Plough ...
Then to the Maids with wheaten Hats;
To the rough sickle, and crookt Scyth,
Drink frollick boyes, till all be blythe."

Clearly in Herrick's time, the late 17th Century, a good time was had by all, the groaning board holding more food than most labouring people would see in a year. Hardy's fine description of the harvest supper given by Bathsheba Everdene in *Far From The Madding Crowd*, is strongly evocative, with its wonderful characterisations of Dorset farming folk and the entertainments they enjoyed.

Other sources give details of harvest celebrations in several Dorset villages, describing dances and songs from Marnhull, and the 'Dance of the Broomsticks' which was performed at Whitchurch Canonicorum. Also quoted are the 'Heel and Toe Dance' from Piddlehinton, and a 'Ring Dance' at Burton Bradstock. At Whitchurch Canonicorum the villagers made 'furmity' after the harvest, which was a mixture of wheat, raisins and currants; this mixture was boiled slowly and sweetened with sugar, then eaten with a

The decorated 'hock-cart' coming in from the fields

A Rural Celebration

spoon like porridge. There are many who have strong suspicions that certain other 'enlivening' ingredients were also added!

In many other parts of the country as well as in Dorset, there are records of a strange ceremony involved with the cutting of the last sheaf of corn. This last cut symbolised the capture of the 'Spirit of the Corn', and the last sheaf was often tied into an animal or 'dolly' shape, the origin of the 'Corn Dollies' or 'Kern Babies' now seen mainly in craft shops. This figure was kept throughout the year for luck and in some places was ploughed into the ground when the first furrow was cut on Plough Monday, to ensure the fertility of that year's crop.

Associated with this last cut was a curious ritual known variously as 'crying the mare', or 'crying the neck' (or 'knack'), in which the men — and later the women, stand in a circle and chant ... "We have 'en'", several times, getting louder each time. On the question being put ... "What do 'ee have?" the reply comes, "A neck! A neck!" Hats are flung in the air — and then there is more drinking and dancing far into the night. This form of the ritual, or something very similar, was practised in Devon, Dorset and Cornwall, and in recent years has been revived by the Old Cornwall Society. Many folklorists have tried to explain the origins of the custom. Udal said that there were very similar customs in Germany, as told by Grimm, in which the god Woden was invoked at the end of harvest, and the last sheaf of corn was left standing, "for Woden's horse". He suggested that "We have 'en'", is a corruption of the Saxon "Woden". As is the case with most ancient customs, it was widely believed that if the people failed to carry out the ritual, then ill-fortune would follow and next year's harvest would be a failure. As the old people died, and their heirs tried to carry out half-remembered and half-understood rituals, it is inevitable that the words should become garbled.

Another widespread custom was for the gang of harvesters to elect a 'Lord and Lady of the Harvest' (the Lady was a man), who would be responsible for leading the work and handling all transactions with the farmer. The labourers could be fined by the Lord for breaches of discipline or laziness. William Barnes too, wrote much on the subject of the harvest and described in detail the food set out for the workers by the farmer's wife and the horns of beer consumed by the merry party at the Harvest Supper. He also quotes the words of an old Dorset song which proposed the health of the farmer ...

"Here's a health unto Maister
The founder of the feast,
And I hope to God with all my heart
His soul in Heaven mid rest;

That everything mid prosper
That ever he teake in hand,
Vor we be all his servants,
And all at his command."

Harvesting near Tolpuddle 1900

Beating the Bounds

A mid-19th Century assembly for Beating the Bounds, led by the Beadle

In the 1930s the boys of the Bluecoat School at Blandford were beaten annually by the Mayor and Aldermen, a practice which was intended "the better to affix the places of town boundary in their minds".

This ancient custom, which still exists, though in diluted form, in many places, has its origins in Roman times, in the festivals dedicated to the god Terminus (of boundaries) and the corn goddess Ceres. Like all the old pagan festivals, the Roman 'Terminalia' and 'Ambarvalia' were later appropriated to Christian ends, becoming a dual-purpose occasion, with both religious and lay elements. Not only were the crops and fields blessed, but the boundaries of the parish were carefully marked out so that they were remembered by all who were present, in a time when no written records were kept.

Before the Reformation, which toned down many of the more elaborate customs, these annual processions were highly ceremonial affairs with Lords of the Manor, their bailiffs, reeves and stewards being present, as well as the clergy and parish officials and most of the local people. Traditionally the processions took place in Rogation Week, that is the three days before Holy Thursday or Ascension Day and sometimes on Ascension Day itself. The processional cross was carried and the parish officials had their staves and banners and other marks of office, while some among the company carried bells or other musical instruments.

The procession would set off from the church and follow closely the bounds of the parish. In order to impress upon those present exactly where the boundaries were, the procession would frequently stop, to sing a psalm here, or say a prayer there. On the way the crops were blessed; here and there the boundary would cross a stream and someone would be thrown in; perhaps by a wall the company would stop for cakes and ale, or by an ancient oak two of the company would dance, or a tune be rung on the bells. But the most well-remembered places were surely those where the 'beatings' took place, from which the custom gets its name. For at certain spots the boys in the parade would get a 'tanning' from the village elders on the seat of their pants, which was no doubt an excellent aid-memoire!

In Dorset almost very parish at one time observed the perambulations in Rogation Week, and the dual nature of the ceremony remained as Brand in his *Popular Antiquities* (1905) stated ..."To beg a blessing on the fruits of the earth and to preserve the rights and properties of the parish".

The perambulation of Melcombe Regis was still being carried out in the 1880s, and an old woman who had taken part 75 years earlier remembered an "old eldern stubb" as part of the boundary. At Cerne 'Thorn Stump' was referred to on the OS map in recent years and records showing the same 'Thorne Stubbe' as a boundary marker go back to 1301. At Radipole when the procession reached the pond, the parson read a chapter of the Bible and a psalm was sung, while at West Lulworth, beer, cake and bread were partaken of at Furzeymill Pitt, at the limit of the parish boundary. There are written accounts also of the village procession at Chideock and also from Marnhull in 1808.

In 1616 there was a court case between two

Impressing the Memory of Small Boys

parishes, Stratton and Charminster, which had been locked in a long dispute. Both had carried out their perambulation, but had used different routes, and the boundaries now appeared to overlap. There was considerable local feeling, shown by the evidence of the Stratton witnesses .. "... The inhabitants of Charminster within this eight and thirty years have altered their course of procession ... and at the first coming of the new curatt ... in his first perambulation in procession dyd forsake their old and wonted way and course ... and did appoynt the said curatt to goe farther in upon Stratton by Fifty acres or thereabouts than they did before, which is the land in variance ... " They also said that the oldest inhabitants had been prevented from attending by threats, for they were the ones who knew where the proper boundaries were.

On the Chesil Beach about four miles along there is a 'Bound Stone' which was, and is regularly visited by the Portland Court Leet officers to preserve their boundary and maintain their parish rights. In recent years there has been revived a 'beating the bounds' ceremony around Poole Harbour and Quay, combined with a Water Carnival. This took place four-yearly and was no doubt a revival of a much older custom. The future of this 'watered-down' ceremony is in doubt at present due to organisational difficulties.

By far the best account of a perambulation of the bounds in Dorset was the report in the *Bath Daily Chronicle* of 24th October 1891, which went into great detail about how the Mayor of Bridport and the 'city fathers' all finished up in the water when trying to cross the millpond on a raft, clearly not strong enough to hold their weight, encumbered as they probably were by heavy chains of office. The report states that "the Mayor promptly described the boundary by swimming ashore ... but the Borough Surveyor remained alone on the raft, and was eventually towed to land completely drenched". Presumably these two at least had no problems remembering where the boundary was.

Boundary stone on the Wilts/Dorset boundary, in the Larmer Tree Grounds

Beating the Bounds at Weymouth 1909

31

The Story Of The Great Diamond

William Pitt (the 'elder') First Earl of Chatham, grandson of Thomas Pitt

In the year 1701 a runaway slave turned up on the coast of India with a huge uncut diamond weighing 410 carats concealed in an open wound in his leg, which must have caused him considerable pain. He sold the gem to an English skipper, who showed his gratitude by murdering him, so the poor slave derived no benefit at all from what Treves called 'a surgical feat of some interest'!

This tall story is connected to the village of Blandford St Mary in Dorset. The person who eventually procured the great gem, Thomas Pitt, was a Dorset man. He was the grandfather of William Pitt. Thomas Pitt was a colourful character and had a chequered career. As a young man he went to sea and was soon running his own successful trading business in competition with the East India company in the Far East. He was constantly in trouble with the East India Company who had the monopoly and would not grant him a licence. The company tried to prevent him trading and fined him £1000 at one stage but he was quite undaunted and became even more successful. Having made a great deal of money he returned home and married Jane Innes, who bore him six children. He bought the Manor at Stratford-sub-Castle near Salisbury and got himself elected as Member of Parliament for Old Sarum. Surprisingly, he was later appointed Governor of Fort St. George in Madras, by his old enemy, the East India Company. There must have been some corruption, for after his appointment, no less than eighteen members of the committee who appointed him were thrown out by enraged shareholders. He must have been a plausible rogue, for somehow he kept the post,

even after this scandal. While he was abroad, news from home revealed that his wife was squandering his hard-won fortune. Pitt wrote several angry letters threatening to cut his wife off — though at the same time he was helping other, less well-off relatives, so meanness was not one of his faults.

There are several versions of the story of the 'Great Diamond', some of them 'very ugly' as one commentator puts it. What is certain is that in 1702 Thomas Pitt had the opportunity to buy this huge stone, no doubt thinking as many others had done before, that with such a prize in his possession all his worries would be over. The diamond was apparently dug in the Parteal mines on the Kistna, in India. Some say that Pitt obtained it by crooked means, Treves says it was by 'a stretch of power'. Others believe that it was legitimately purchased through an agent, from the proprietor of the mine. After much bargaining, Pitt paid the equivalent of £20,400 for it.

His son Robert is said to have brought the diamond home to England, perhaps concealed in his shoe. For the next fifteen years the massive diamond was Pitt's 'great concern'. What to do with it? Where to get the best price for it? In an extravagant marketing exercise, Thomas Pitt had crystal models made of the stone, which were sent to the Kings of France, Spain, and Persia, and also to the Prince of Wales, in an attempt to find a buyer. Finally the French Government began negotiations and Pitt was told to take the jewel to the Court Jewellers in France, a deposit of £40,000 being lodged in London by the French, who were going to purchase the diamond on behalf of the Regent for the King of France. The price was to be £125,000, in addition to the

Blandford St Mary Church

£40,000 already on deposit. Pitt would receive part of the French Crown Jewels as security for the balance. It is not known if he received the balance, but it is certain that he made good profit, for he said at the time, "I have received a third of the money and four parcels of Crown Jewels."

The cost of cutting the huge diamond was £5,000 and the chips alone yielded £8,000. After cutting, the final size of the stone was 137 carats; (the famous Koh-i-Noor is 102 carats) and it was set in the French Crown for the Coronation of Louis XV in 1722. In 1791, the National Assembly ordered that the jewel should be sold along with other gems. It was placed on view to the public, and was immediately stolen, but was recovered a year later. In 1804 the stone was set in the hilt of the Sword of State for the Coronation of the Emperor Napoleon. It has been in the possession of the Louvre in Paris since 1887.

Thomas Pitt devoted the rest of his life to politics. With the money from the diamond, which had become known as the 'Pitt' or 'Regent' Diamond, he bought property at Woodyates near Sixpenny Handley and at Chettle near Blandford, as well as other property in Cornwall and Berkshire. When he died in 1726, his body was brought back to Blandford St Mary to be buried. The legal battles over his property continued for many years after his death. Ironically, Napoleon, whose sword at last bore the great diamond, was the arch-enemy of Pitts grandson, William, when he was Prime Minister. Thomas Pitt is remembered, inevitably, as 'Diamond Pitt' and is generally thought to have been a scoundrel

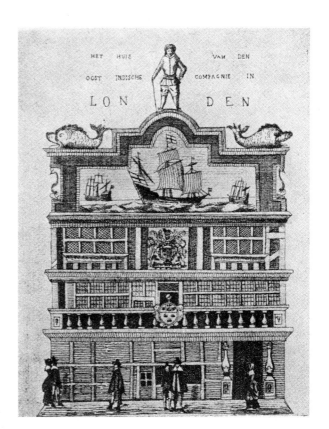

East India House, Leadenhall Street, London. The company had a monopoly of trade between England and the far East in 18th.Cent.

if not an outright crook — though a Latin inscription on a tablet in the tiny church where he is buried praises his many virtues.

Whether the beautiful diamond brought happiness to either Pitt or the Emperor Napoleon is open to question.

St Andrew's Church, Trent

ALL FLESH IS GRASSE AND THE GLORY OF IT IS AS THE FLOVRE OF THE FIELDE.

This curious inscription is painted in reverse over an elegant arch in Trent Church, as a monument to the wife of Thomas Gerard, the early Dorset historian, who wrote *A Survey of Dorsetshire* in 1732 under the name of the Rev. John Coker. His wife was a member of the Coker family of Mappowder. The arch separates the Gerard, Manor or North Chapel from the nave of the tiny church. The significance of the backward writing is unknown, but it has been suggested that if the attention of any young ladies in the congregation should stray from the sermon, and they should begin to peep into their mirrors, this text would remind them that earthly beauty does not last!

The tiny, golden village of Trent can have changed little since Gerard's day. Hamstone cottages line the winding street and a raised flagstone pathway runs along the whole length, by a stone wall topped with fragrant wallflowers and tumbling aubretia. Little traffic passes this way and the place seems lost in a drowsy vision of times gone by. Trent (the name means a river liable to flood), has been a place of human habitation from earliest times. The village was once part of Somerset, being only a few miles outside Yeovil; but since the end of the last century has been included in Dorset. The most famous visitor to the village was Charles II, when on the run, for it was here, in the Manor House that he was concealed by Colonel Wyndham in 1651.

The little church is a delightful building with a steeple, one of only three in the whole county. Built of Ham Hill stone, quarried less than a dozen miles away, it was once the property of the Priory of Studley in Warwickshire. The Priory made a present of its oldest bell which is dated 1370. There are a number of items to interest the visitor, apart from the reversed writing over the arch — in the porch is a sign ...

"All persons are requested to take off Pattens and Clogs before entering the Church."

This reflects the times when villagers had to walk long distances in all weathers to get to church, from the outlying farmsteads and hamlets. The oldest part of the church is the nave, part of which dates from the early 13th century, as does one ancient window. The 15th century screen is believed to have been carved by the monks at Glastonbury. One thing which took my fancy was the decorative finish on the walls of the chancel. This has an all-over plasterwork, embossed floral design, giving a rich textured appearance. The darkly ancient pews date from before the Reformation, and represent a masterpiece of early 15th century carving. Several pew-ends are carved with the traditional symbols of the Passion, including the 'sacred heart', the nails, the crown of thorns, the scourge and a ladder, together with other symbols. The striking thing is that when the pews are 'read' in the correct order, they spell out the hidden message, known to Christians the world over ...

'Ave maria, gratia plena Dominus tecum. Amen."

("Hail Mary, full of grace. The Lord be with you. Amen.")

The local tradition is that when Cromwell's soldiers were approaching, bent on destroying all church possessions which showed the smal-

The 14th Century Chantry House

lest hint of Catholicism, the villagers panicked and took down the pews and their Latin prayer, mixing their positions up so that the message could not be read. The pews stayed mixed up until fairly recently times, when the group was restored to its original place. The Trent people had good reason to fear for their church, for Cromwell's men had orders from the 'Committee for the Demolishing of Monuments of Superstition and Idolatry', which was set up in 1643. The artefacts to be destroyed included "crosses and crucifixes, images inside or outside the church, every altar or table of stone, also tapers, candlesticks and basons from the Communion table".

Trent Church was dedicated to St Andrew, or the Blessed Virgin Mary. The village 'feast' was observed on the first Sunday after the Assumption of the Virgin, the 15th August.

By the entrance to the church stands a sturdy 14th century house, beautifully preserved and unmodernised. This is the 'Chantry House'. Chantries were religious foundations, usually consisting of a small chapel attached to a church endowed by a wealthy person who wished his memory to be perpetuated after his death by the saying of Mass for himself and his family. The priest who said these Masses would live in the Chantry house. The house at Trent was built in the early 15th century under the will of John Franks who was Master of the Rolls in 1428 and a native of the village. He died in 1437, leaving £7-6s-8d annual stipend for the chantry Chaplain. There is speculation that the figure of a 'judge' in Trent Church is John Franks, but the sources do not agree on this. The Chantry Chapel was probably under the tower, where there is evidence

of infilling, and the outline of a piscina is visible. Here also is a 'squint' to the High altar and a separate door by which the Chantry priest could enter the Church.

The history of Trent with its tales of bottomless pools, hiding places for kings, and secret messages, have given the people of the village a very keen sense of mystery. My aunt, now 80, who lived in the Chantry House in the 1930s, says that she is convinced that there was a secret passage from the house to the church, for inside the house can be seen the traces of an old doorway. Outside, near the back door of the Chantry House, which opens into the churchyard, can be seen a stone which could very easily be the lintel of the entrance to a sunken passage.

St Andrew's Church, Trent

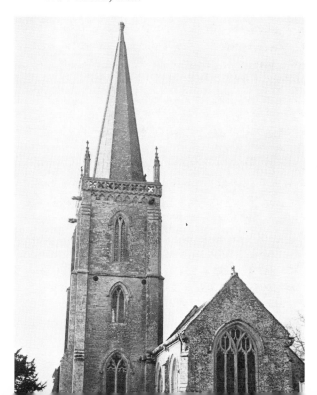

The Larmer Tree Grounds

Shades of the Orient can be found in the farthest reaches of Dorset, in a deeply wooded glade, thronged with peacocks and with gold and silver pheasants, who strut between an Indian Pavilion and a Classical temple, pecking incongruously between the richly carved boards of an Oriental bandstand. Nearby is an imposing open-air theatre of classical design.

This unusual setting can be found on the Rushmore Estate which straddles the border between Dorset and Wiltshire. These pleasure grounds are the quaintly named 'Larmer Tree Grounds', laid out in the 1880s by the well-known Dorset archaeologist, General Augustus Henry Lane Fox Pitt-Rivers. The General devoted the last twenty years of his life to carrying out extensive archaeological digs on Cranborne Chase and the surrounding areas. He collected huge numbers of Stone-age and early Iron-age relics and artefacts, which he bestowed on various museums. He was really the first archaeologist to use scientific methods of excavation, for earlier enthusiasts had often tended to destroy more than they unearthed. He set up his own museum at Farnham in a building which, in the 1850s had been used in an attempt to set up a school for Gypsy children. The gypsy children did not appear for the school, and the experiment was deemed a failure. He turned the building into a fine museum, with many exhibits from Martin Down, the Romano-British village at Woodcutts, and from Bokerley Dyke. The contents of this museum are now held at Oxford. By all authorities Pitt-Rivers is regarded as one of the foremost contributors to archaeological work in Dorset.

In 1880, when he inherited the Rivers estates, the General began to put another far-sighted but somewhat eccentric plan into operation, and the grounds, called the 'Larmer Tree Grounds' from very early times, were an ideal place for that plan. One theory states that the name came from the idea of an 'Alarum Tree', where in Saxon times a horn was sounded to bring the tribesmen together. The original tree stood on the actual boundary between the two counties, and was the spot where King John used to meet his huntsmen when staying at nearby Tollard Royal. The old tree was a wych elm, long since dead and only a fragment now remains which is bound to a new, vigorous oak. Centuries ago the Cranborne Chase Courts were held under the Larmer tree and here were settled all matters relating to the Chase and to forest rights.

The grounds are still very beautiful. Tall trees surround the central lawns and winding rhododendron walks thread their paths through the undergrowth. Behind the little classical temple, built in 1880, a flight of stone steps leads down to a now unkempt, sunken garden. A tinkle of running water falls into a small pool where two delightful bronze cranes are poised on a tiny island in the centre. Huge hydrangeas and other overgrown shrubs line the grass walks which lead to a small, rustic summer-house called Temple View.

The classical temple is very small, only about eight feet in diameter, with a perfect domed roof. It was clearly plastered pink at some stage. Inside is a mosaic floor and a sunburst-painted ceiling under the dome. Across the lawn is a richly-carved Oriental bandstand with two storeys and a smaller Indian pavilion with similar white walls and

The 'classical temple', built in 1880

a black timber frame. The pavilion faces a huge classical stage with its arched proscenium. The inside is painted in delicate atmospheric style as a permanent backdrop. Hidden deep in the woods is a tea-room which once provided refreshments for visitors.

For these charming grounds were not laid out for the pleasure of the General himself, but as an attraction for the public. The General's ideas were far-reaching and largely philanthropic. Visitors could stroll in the grounds daily until dusk, with bands playing and refreshments laid on. Crockery and stoves were provided for the picnic areas and certain 'Quarters', with seats and tables could be booked for private parties. Meals could be provided by arrangement. The caretaker and staff wore quaint green velvet uniforms based on those of the Chase keepers in former times. General Pitt Rivers thought of everything ...

> "Swings, skittles and bowls will be found for the amusement of those who soon grow tired of Art and Nature ... Races and sports are held in September in the survival of annual hunt that took place here up to the end of the last century. This rarely public-spirited owner laid out a pleasure garden which in populous districts would be inundated by visitors and even in this out of the way situation attracts many thousands."

The General's eccentric plan included the various exotic animals which roamed the park, including reindeer, llamas, Indian cattle, and yaks, while the various 'Quarters' were named after 'Owls, Yaks, Hogs, Hounds and Cats'. The attractive buildings, bought at great expense from an exhibition at Earl's Court, were filled with Oriental treasures for the public to admire, while the unique statue which graced the grounds also drew many admirers. This was Boehm's 'Hunter of Early Days' and featured a Celt mounted on a shaggy pony. Alas the statue can no longer be seen.

General Pitt Rivers died in 1900 and was buried at Tollard Royal, where a fine marble memorial is set in the wall of the church tower. He was certainly a remarkable man and his memory lives on.

The open-air theatre

The Indian pavilion

Rites of Spring

Morris dancers with hobby horse, friar, a fool and a minstrel

"That was not the end of the dancing. Enthusiasts returned to the rectory barn and danced till dark to the strains of a fiddle, supported perhaps by a flute; and then they retired to the Ox Inn and danced with unabated energy till daylight of the following morning."

Such gaiety was a normal feature of May Day in the village of Shillingstone two hundred years ago, and was shared in many a Dorset village of the time.

Every culture in the world has its Spring Festival, the origins often long-forgotten. In Roman times the Spring festival was called 'Floralia', and was dedicated to the goddess Flora. Green boughs and flowers were brought in to decorate homes, which shows the origin of the custom of 'Bringing in the May', so beloved by country folk. The most well-known symbol of May festivities is of course the Maypole, but its origins do not go back that far, for it is first found in a written source in 1504 in Reading. From that time on, the cult of the Maypole progressed. Its history was somewhat chequered, for there were always those who did not approve. In the 16th century every town and village indulged in riotous 'May-games', 'Church Ales' and other joyful celebrations of the coming of Spring. Stubbes in 1583 described the typical village Maypole ...

".. covered all over with flowers and hearbes, bounde rounde aboute with stringes, from the top to the bottom, and some tyme painted with variable colours."

At Cerne, a long-standing tradition states that the Maypole was erected in the Trendle, the earthwork above the head of the Giant, but some sources dispute this and insist that the Maypole was always set up in the village. At Cattistock, the Maypole was set up opposite the village pub, and the custom did not die out finally till 1835, when it was reportedly difficult to find money to pay for musicians. As late as the first decade of this century, my uncle remembers the Maypole being carried in procession through the village of Trent, before being set up ready for the festivities.

According to William Barnes, Shillingstone was the last Dorset village to keep up 'the tall token of a merry May Day', as he called it. He goes on to say ....

"And Shillingston, that on her height
Shows up her tower to op'ning day,
And high-shot Maypole, yearly dight
With flow'ry wreaths of merry May."

For the Maypole at Shillingstone was the tallest in all Dorset, although the May games were not actually held until June 9th, and appear to have been combined with the celebrations for Oak Apple Day on the 29th May. This also coincided with the date of a medieval fair around the time of St. Barnabas' Day, the 11th. The tall pole was garlanded with Spring flowers and the dancing went on all night. There were also booths and stalls, with cheap-jacks selling trinkets and sweetmeats. Here also Mummer's plays survived, and the Shillingstone Bull, something like the famous Dorset 'Ooser', was still in existence, to frighten the girls, up to the 1890s. 'Jack-in-the-Green' was a prominent figure in many Dorset celebrations. He was a person dressed from head to toe in green leaves and branches, which were fixed to a wooden frame, so that he walked along in-

Maypoles, Garlands and Robin Hood

side it. Modern folklorists suppose that Jack-in-the-Green was a descendant of a tree-god, or a woodland sprite, but his origins are obscure. This figure reappears over and over again in folklore and legend, and his smiling face is even seen in Church carvings, with scrolls of foliage issuing from his mouth. At the May games, Jack-in-the-Green was interchangeable with Robin Hood, that other elusive woodland character, and where this was the case, as at Bridport and Lyme Regis, Robin Hood and Maid Marian were King and Queen of the May. At Lyme, Robin was attended by his 'Merry Men', all dressed in green with leafy crowns. The girls attending Maid Marian wore primrose crowns and led a flower-bedecked cow, with gilded horns.

Another important feature of May Day and Spring festivals were flower garlands, carried round by the children at Sherborne, Wyke Regis and Swyre and Puncknowle. At Abbotsbury, Garland day is still held on May 13th, Old May Day, and the garlands are taken round the village, and then into the church for a service. In former times the garlands were flung into the sea in a 'blessing' ceremony.

All this fun and frolicking was in full swing in the 15th and 16th Centuries, until the Reformation, and still later the Puritans stamped out any local functions which seemed to smack of 'popery'. That the rustic celebrations often led to drunkenness and licentious behaviour was a further cause for concern. The much-loved custom of 'Bringing in the May' was roundly condemned by Stubbes in 1583. Calling the Maypole a 'stinckyng idoll', he went on to say that he had heard ...

".. credibly reported .. by men of great gravitie and reputation, that of fortie, threescore, or a hundred maides going to the wood overnight, there have scarcely the third part of them returned home again undefiled."

Later historians have cast much doubt on Stubbes' inferences, suggesting that the young people of those days were no different than young people of any other time, and that the real reason for the Puritan clamp-down was that the processions and communal festivities were based on Catholic practices.

Many attempts were made in more recent times to re-start the May games, but such revivals are seldom successful, alas the continuity is broken. Today Morris dancers can often be seen at May fairs, and the 'May Queen' or 'May Princess' is often crowned to lead the fun, while village children trip sedately round a tiny Maypole — in a somewhat feeble imitation of the former vigorous and lively expression of the age-old Rites of Spring.

Children take round their May garland, asking for pennies

Underground Passages and Tunnels

John Trenchard sat in his favourite spot on a tomb in the little churchyard of East Fleet. Looking down, he noticed a crack had opened at the base of the slab, and a dark hole tempted him to explore. He was soon terrified and scrambled out of the darkness in a panic, resolving to come back with a light to explore the tunnel properly, tempted by dreams of hidden treasure. This is *Moonfleet* by John Meade Faulkner, a well-loved Dorset book, first published in 1898 and devoted to the enthralling pursuit of smuggling — a Dorset pastime practiced by many in former times.

The coast along the Fleet area, and the remote bays of St Gabriel's and Charmouth were ideal for smuggling — and the rugged coast paths made pursuit difficult. There were plenty of hiding places along the way including several churches, and also, if all the tales are to be believed, hollow tombstones in certain graveyards and specially constructed vaults at remote farmhouses. Passages and tunnels have been found in several places as well as the one under the tiny East Fleet church in which John Trenchard began his hair-raising adventure. Here the Mohun family vault was part of the complex of passages used by the team of smugglers to hide their booty.

At Chaldon Herring there was a passage under the pub, the *Sailor's Return*, leading to the house behind and another under the fields between the Inn and the church; perhaps the landlord of the pub and the vicar were both involved? At Charlton Marshall there were two old cottages facing each other, one of which was called 'Wayside Cottage'. There was said to be an underground passage between the two cottages under the road, and also one of the cottages had a secret room.

At Sturminster Newton there was a supposed tunnel from Sturminster Castle to the Mill where barrels of brandy were said to have been stored after coming up the Stour by boat. The tunnel is said to have been made in the Middle Ages by the inhabitants of the castle who were afraid of attack. Fiddleford Farm was also said to be a depot for smuggled goods, for the strings of pack ponies which would have come inland on moonless nights from Lulworth and other quiet places on the coast. Hutchins was the first to throw doubt on the truth of the Sturminster legends, for he said that part of the castle was pulled down in 1732, and that the Stour is barely navigable anyway. The rest of the castle was pulled down in 1840, so it could not have been in use for long as part of the smuggling network, if at all.

At Kinson lived the most famous Dorset smuggler, Isaac Gulliver (1745-1816). His house at East Howe, called 'Howe Lodge' was said to have had an underground passage leading into the cellars. A small door high up in an open chimney in the cellar led to a secret room above, which was a hiding place for fugitives from the law. Other 'hidey-holes' and a well also existed in this house, for Gulliver was a professional smuggler, and a successful one at that. The building was pulled down in 1958.

The old *Five Bells Inn* at Morcombelake, later burnt down, had a false window-seat with a deep hole under it for hiding contraband goods. Smuggling was a profitable business and many otherwise respectable citizens were involved in it one way or another. The number of hiding places for both goods and people, and the tricks that were

Wool Manor, across the water-meadows from Bindon Abbey

Smuggled Brandy and Fugitive Priests

used to outwit the Customs and Excise men, show that it was a well-organised and carefully planned operation. It involved landing goods on dark and lonely beaches, storing them in caves or underground vaults — then transporting them by pack-pony over land at dead of night across rough and rugged trackways, with further bolt-holes conveniently placed along the way. It was a risky business. Accomplices were paid in kind and many farmers in remote spots, and even churchmen with empty vaults became part of the network. Specially constructed underground vaults have been found at farms in the Corscombe and Halstock area and near Lambert's Castle. In one place near Halstock there was a 'paved pond', so that kegs of brandy could be easily raised from the water.

Another group of underground passages and tunnels are to be found in the Monasteries and Abbeys of Dorset, though in many cases it would appear that these were probably part of the drainage systems, for monasteries were usually sited near streams and thus running water could be brought into the buildings. However this cannot have been the case at Cerne, where an underground tunnel connects the Abbey with 'Cat-and-Chapel Hill' (where now the road runs to Piddletrenthide). Perhaps the monks had a passage to get to the little chapel which once stood on top of the hill. At Milton there were a number of passages, one of which led to Winterborne Houghton church, and thence to the old tithe barn at Winterborne Clenston. Legend says that these tunnels were used by the monks. Yet another tunnel led from Milton Abbey to Quarleston Farm and another to Delcombe Manor. These

tunnels would have been about 2 miles long, and would have entailed a great deal of work to construct — it is hard to believe that the monks would have undertaken such a task.

At Forde Abbey there was said to be a tunnel from the Abbey to Hay Farm which also had a 'priest's hole'. This leads one to suspect that it might have been constructed later, in times of Catholic persecution, rather than in the time of the monks. A long tradition states that there is a tunnel from Woolbridge Manor to Bindon Abbey, now a ruin. This is another story which is hard to believe, as the ground between the two is largely water-meadow and the tunnel would have to run under numerous water-courses, making construction very difficult. Shaftesbury Abbey had several supposed tunnels, which have been uncovered at various times during the course of excavations. As Laura Sydenham says, "unfortunately, there is never a reliable eye-witness to vouch for the truth of such tales."

Sturminster Newton mill

Bribery and Corruption

The town of Shaftesbury had a reputation for three things ...

"More strong beer than water,
The churchyard higher than the church;
And more rogues than honest men."

The first is a reference to the fact that Shaftesbury had considerable problems in the regular supply of water, being built on a hilltop; the second refers to the fact that the church of St. John the Baptist, once at the top of St. John's Hill, had a churchyard which was used by the people of St. James', at the bottom of the hill, and the third, well, the third speaks for itself, doesn't it? Certainly there are one or two episodes in its history of which Shaftesbury must be less than proud, but by today's standards, it was certainly no worse than many other towns. Possibly one of the incidents which gave rise to this unfortunate slur on the town and its inhabitants would have been the case of Sir Osbert Gifford, excommunicated by the Archbishop of Canterbury when he visited Shaftesbury, for the offence of stealing two nuns out of the Nunnery at Wilton in 1225. As well as being excommunicated, Sir Osbert had to suffer several other humiliating punishments as well. He was forbidden ever to enter a Nunnery or be in the company of nuns again — and then for three Sundays he was to be stripped and whipped publicly in the Parish Church at Wilton and in the Market-Place, and then again in the Parish Church of Shaftesbury. He was also to fast for some months, not wear a shirt for three years — not to take the title of Knight — or wear any colour except russet with sheepskin garments. The nuns were to be restored to the Nunnery and would receive similar punishment. All of which Sir Os-bert pledged himself to do, on oath. Treves suggests that the nuns were probably the prettiest at Wilton, and also that they were probably willing accomplices.

Treves says that after the Dissolution of the Abbey 'this cheery hill town fell upon evil days. No longer a burial place for Kings and Queens, no longer the goal of eager pilgrimage nor the rendezvous of nobles, it took in despair to the making of shirt buttons. At this it fared somewhat indifferently, for in one petition the burgesses plead "the Towne has grown about £200 in debte: there are above 300 begging people to be relieved and there are not above 30 householders in all the towne able to give relieffe".' So perhaps it was poverty that was really the problem, and which caused the townspeople to be sometimes less than honest. For after the demise of the Abbey, there was no official body able to support the poor, and its wide-ranging 'social services' were not taken up by anyone else.

Another scandalous episode is concerned with bribery, corruption and even conspiracy. From the reign of Elizabeth up to 1832 the town was represented by two Members of Parliament. The right to elect the members belonged to the Mayor and certain landowners, though in practice it was usually the most powerful Lord of the Manor who elected the representatives. After the Dissolution, which split up many of the larger land-holdings, individual Lords of the Manor owned less and less property, but still continued to claim the right to elect the Members of Parliament. Usually their candidates were accepted by the townspeople. Very often generous bribes were given to facilitate the process, for it was commonplace in the

Lady Blaize in her 'state barge', on Election Day 1781, with farcical attendants

country at that time to reward faithful voters with gifts of money. It is not surprising that the poor voters of Shaftesbury took the money. As one historian comments, "It was a convenient and comfortable arrangement for all".

But in 1773, a group of more honest and perhaps wealthier townspeople nominated their own candidate, Hans Wintrop Mortimer. He was defeated and the candidates championed by the Lords of the Manor were elected. These were Francis Sykes and Thomas Rumbold. But both were expelled two years later, accused of bribery, and Mortimer was installed in their stead. Exactly the same thing happened in 1779, and again Mortimer was seated instead of the rigged candidate. Rumbold had received a large sum of money for damages in the bribery case and so he bought as many properties in the town as he could hoping to use this as a lever to secure more votes. However a rival did the same, which brought about a disgraceful display of trickery and fraud to gain their evil ends. Both pulled out all the stops culminating in a farcical situation in which two 'Nabobs', which Darton explains as "persons suitably enriched at the expense of India" were returned to Parliament in what was later described as an example of 'shameless venality'. This is what happened, as told by Treves ...

> "... a person concealed under a fantasical disguise and called by the name of Punch was placed in a small apartment, and through a hole in the door delivered out to the voters parcels containing twenty guineas; upon which they were conducted to another apartment in the same house, where they found a person called Punch's secretary, and signed notes for the value, but which was made payable to an imaginary character to whom they had given the name of Glenbucket."

Punch, it appears, was no less a person than one Matthews, an Alderman. Treves goes on

> "... He would have been long and fondly remembered by the voters of Shaftesbury, for the vision of parcels containing twenty gold coins dropping through a hole in a door into eager palms is pleasant to dwell upon."

Treves knows human nature as well as he knows the highways and byways of Dorset!

An Election scene in the 18th century

43

Kill or Cure

"Get an honest lawyer's pocket hand-
    kerchief,
Wash it in an honest miller's millpond —
Dry it, and iron it with an honest tailor's
    goose,
It you can do this you will never have
    toothache again."

Judging by this tongue-in-cheek rhyme from
North Dorset, it would seem that toothache was
the one thing no quack could cure.

Until the development of scientific medicine
during the last 150 years or so, all medical practice had been firmly plant-based, and contained
strong elements of magical and superstitious practice. In the Middle-ages it was a commonplace
thing for poor folk to consult the village herb-
woman, or the quack bone-setter who travelled
the countryside. Cures were often in the form of
plant-based medicine, such as a comfrey poultice
or horehound tea, and very often in the form of
charms, which usually involved a secret message
or form of words, not always written down —
to be used by the patient as prescribed by the
practitioner. If the instructions, which perhaps included 'gathering leaves by moonlight', or 'turning round three times as the cock crowed', were
not followed to the letter, the charm would not
work. The practitioners traded on such mystique,
and it is small wonder that many became known as
witches.

William Barnes in his 'Fore-say' to Udal's
book, *Dorsetshire Folklore*, remarked on how
prevalent the use of spells was in Dorset, and
explained the term ..."... charms and spells have

seemingly always been a share of the folklore of
Dorset, as of all England. A charm (Saxon-'cyrm')
is by its first meaning a mingled sound of voices of
men or birds, and in folklore it seems to mean a
form of muttered words — and a spell was — 'a
form of words', and then also a message".

Some of the instructions for charms are, to say
the least, bizarre. This charm to cure toothache is
quoted by Udal ...
"Cut a slit in a young oak tree. Cut off a bit of
your hair and push it under the bark. Put your
hand on the tree and say, "This I bequeath to the
oak tree, in the name of the Father, the Son and
the Holy Ghost. Amen." As we see, it is almost a
prayer, and embodies an inextricable mix of magic
and miracle.

For boils, the sufferer should creep under the
arch where a bramble touches the ground, then
creep through, three mornings in a row, against
the rising sun. For rupture, an infant should be
passed through a slit cut in a young ash tree, nine
times — and then the tree should be bound up
tightly — as the tree heals, so will the rupture. For
epilepsy, some crockery should be stolen from
a minister, pounded up and then given to the
patient as a medicinal powder. For cramp the
shoes should be placed in a 'T' shape before going
to bed. For whooping cough, nine hairs should be
taken from the cross on the back of a white
she-ass, put in a silk bag and worn round the
neck. Clearly there are, in several of these charms,
religious invocations involved as well as the use of
the magical numbers three and nine. The charms
for warts are numerous, and almost all take the
form of rubbing some substance, usually stolen,
on the warts. After this, the meat, or bread is then

Country Cures and Remedies

A toad in a bag, a cure for many different ailments!

buried. As the matter rots, the warts are said to disappear.

Sore eyes were best cured by a visit to one of the many Holy Wells in Dorset, perhaps St Wite's at Morcombelake, or St Augustine's Well at Cerne, also known as the 'Silver Well'. The cure was most effective if the eyes were bathed as soon as the early morning rays of the sun had fallen on the water.

Plant remedies were as common in Dorset as anywhere else — comfrey being a favourite salve for all life's ills. Its country name was 'knit-bone'. Moule quotes a source which states that the red-flowered variety should be used for men, and the white for women. The houseleek was said to be good for 'cooling the blood', while celandine was made into a lotion for piles, indeed its alternative name was pile-wort, from its cluster of bulbous roots. 'Upalong and Downalong' quotes many plant folk remedies, among them cowslip ointment which was said to be very good for the skin, as was any lotion or cream made from elderflowers. Goose-grease was a sovereign remedy for chest ailments, and even today local pensioners can remember being sewn into goose-grease 'undervests' for the winter.

The animal world too was often involved with the making of medicines, snail liquor being used for various ailments, especially chesty coughs. Hare's or rabbit's brains were given to calm down troublesome infants. For jaundice, Udal quotes a most disgusting cure which is worse than the illness ... "Take nine lice, put them on a piece of bread and butter and eat slowly".

One of Dorset's most famous doctors was a 'cunning man' or white witch known as Dr Buck-

land. He lived in the neighbourhood of Lydlinch or Pulham in the 1830s or 40s. DNHAFC *Proceedings*, vol 35 tells how he held a 'Twoad Fair' every May at the change of the moon. He was famous for his cure of the King's Evil (scrofula) and tubercular or running sores. His favourite, and it seems his only, method of treatment was to cut off the head of a toad, put it in a muslin bag and place it next to the patient's skin under the clothes. It was said that if the patient could bear the cold and clammy object, and not mind its 'scrabblen' then he would be cured, but if it made him sick or faint he would die. Dorothy Gardiner in *Companion into Dorset* says that Dr Buckland dressed in white, and that he was assisted by his three daughters, also in white. 'Upalong and Downalong' says he used live toads and that he was well-known to the people of Sturminster Newton, particularly for cases of 'overlooking' or Evil Eye. He clearly took the whole thing very seriously, and was certainly famous far and wide — and probably very rich!

> THE NATIONAL TRUST
> ## ST. WITE'S WELL
> THIS SPRING HAS BEEN KNOWN AS A HOLY WELL SINCE AT LEAST THE 17TH CENTURY. IT IS CONSIDERED TO HAVE CURATIVE PROPERTIES FOR EYE COMPLAINTS. THERE IS A POSSIBLE CONNECTION BETWEEN THE WELL AND THE 13TH CENTURY SHRINE ATTRIBUTED TO ST. WITE IN THE PARISH CHURCH OF WHITCHURCH CANONICORUM, ONE MILE TO THE NORTH.

St Wite's Well, good for sore eyes

The Game of Fives

At Fordington near Dorchester in the late 17th Century eight people were reported for "playing at a game with a Ball called fives in the Churchyard, and thereby have broken the glasse of one of the windows of the church, the reparation thereof is unto the value of five shillings."

Cases like this were by no means uncommon in the days when country folk enjoyed themselves in rough pleasures and pastimes, without the benefit of the special playing areas and safety measures we have today. The situation in nearby Somerset was even worse, there was "fighting and swearing in the churchyard. The church tower was damaged and the windows broken. Bystanders were hit on the head by pieces of stone falling as the players climbed up the buttresses to retrieve their balls." The problem was that it was difficult to find walls high enough and wide enough for this particular game, the flat walls of the local church tower often providing the most suitable area in the locality. Naturally this often led to trouble and at Martock in Somerset, a workman was paid 3/6d to dig a ditch preventing further destruction. Martock Church tower still bears the marks made by the fives players who cut footholds to make it easier to climb up. A flat stone called the 'Hopping stone' was set into the ground 15 feet or so away from the wall. Here also can still be seen the series of scoring holes in the golden sandstone at the side of tower.

The exact origins of the game are unknown. It would seem from historical accounts that it probably evolved from the old game of 'hand-tennis', which was the early forerunner of tennis with rac-quets as we know it today. As early as the 14th century a line called the 'cord' was traced upon a wall, below which the ball-stroke was 'faulty'. At first it was played with the bare hand, and later with a glove — there are some similarities with the game of Pelota, played by the Basques. In fact *The Poulett Arms* at Hinton St George in Somerset has a wall once used for the game, which is known as the 'Pelota Wall', so this may not be far from the truth. There are no records of the rules of the game, but we know there was a referee, and that the players had to bounce the ball in a certain way on a certain portion of the wall. It was apparently a game of great skill, and bets were laid, with men playing for a dinner, or for a sum of money.

In Dorset we know there was a *Fives Court Inn* at Bridport, but this is no longer visible, having been obscured by building. The game was certainly played at Milton Abbas on Fair days and no doubt at other times too. As the game was so widespread in nearby Somerset, it is reasonable to suppose that it was played in most parts of Dorset too, on high days and holidays.

Hone's Everyday Book, published in 1827, recounts the story of the all-time fives 'champion', a man called John Cavanagh from St Giles in London, so we know that the game was much more than just a local, west country affair. Hone comments .. "It may be said that there are things of more importance than striking a ball against a wall .... but it is the finest exercise for the body and the best relaxation for the mind". He goes on to describe the play of the great Cavanagh ...

"His eye was certain, his hand fatal, his presence of mind complete and he always knew exactly what to do. He saw the whole

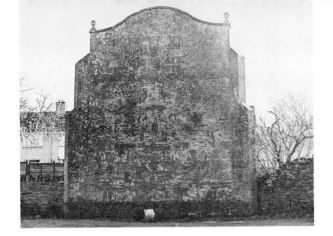

The 'Fives Wall' at the Fleur de Lys, Stoke-sub-Hamdon, Somerset

game and played it, took instant advantage of his adversary's weakness, and recovered balls, as if by a miracle and from sudden thought, that everyone gave for lost. He had equal power and skill, quickness and judgement. He could either outwit his antagonist by finesse, or beat him by main strength. Sometimes when he seemed preparing to send the ball with the full swing of his arm, he would, by a slight turn of the wrist, drop it within an inch of the line. In general, the ball came from his hand, as if from a racket, in a strait horizontal line, so that it was in vain to attempt to overtake or stop it."

The audience, which must have included the enthusiastic Hone, paid half a crown a head to sit in the gallery to watch this scintillating performance.

Down in Somerset, the landlord of the *Fleur de Lys* at Stoke-sub Hamdon built a special fives wall, a handsome construction of Ham Hill stone, about thirty feet high with a graceful line to the design of the top edge, surmounted by elegant finials at the corners. He built a grandstand and often took as much as £60 in gate money. No doubt he sold large quantities of the local cider as well.

For some reason the game of fives declined in popularity and finally disappeared around 1850. There is little evidence now to be seen, and we must rely on the likes of Hone to throw light on the past. Here he tells of a game in Hampshire, watched by Queen Elizabeth I, in which two teams of five men each (is that the origin of the name?) played something which is certainly akin to both fives and tennis ....

..."ten of his Lordship's servants, all Somerset men, in a square greene court before Her Majesty's windowe, did hang up lines, squaring out the forme of a tennis court, and making a cross line in the middle; in this square, they, being stripped to their doublets, played five to five with handball at bord and cord, as they tearme it, to the great liking of Her Highness."

The 'Pelota Wall' at the Poulett Arms, Hinton St George, Somerset

47

The Legend of St. Gabriel's

A strange tale of unknown origin tells how a shipwrecked mariner was washed ashore on the Dorset coast. In dire danger he prayed to the Angel Gabriel to save him and his dying bride. He alone was saved and with the help of a great throng of people who appeared apparently from nowhere, a tiny chapel was built on the remote hillside and dedicated to St. Gabriel.

The tiny stone ruin of St. Gabriel's church still stands on the eastern flank of Golden Cap. Here the landscape sweeps down to the gap in the cliffs called St. Gabriel's mouth and the patchwork of fields and farms, criss-crossed by sunken lanes and little wooded valleys, with here and there an isolated farm or cottage, remains unspoilt and little changed in hundreds of years. A sunken lane, once used by smugglers, leads from the shore inland a short distance to the site of the lost village of Stanton St. Gabriel. A little way up the steep path that leads to the summit of Golden Cap lies the ruined church. There is little left to see. The square form of the tiny nave has been re-pointed and a gate has been fitted to keep out the cows. Lying around are a few sculpted stones, once part of decorative columns and arches. The only building nearby is the old farmhouse, now converted to holiday homes. Golden Cap looms against the sky, and the view across Lyme Bay is magnificent. Frederick Treves' description is the most evocative . . .

....."Close to the farm and encumbered with its litter are the ruins of the village church. Of the tiny sanctuary four grey, ivy-covered walls survive, together with a porch, two arched doorways and certain windows. Within the enclosure is a waste of brambles and thistles. The oppressive silence of the roofless aisle is broken by the cawing of crows and by the splash of the waves on the shore. The east end of the church is the least ruinous. Here is clearly shown the site of the altar, while just in front of the altar is a wild rose bush in blossom. It would seem as if the spirit of the last bride who knelt upon the chancel steps still lived in the blushing petals which the sea wind scatters over the stones."

The earliest reference to a church on this site is a mention in an Ordnance of the Bishop of Salisbury dated Christmas Day 1240. The church served the village of Stanton St. Gabriel, which had a population of just twenty-three families in 1650. The population later declined, and when the coast road from Bridport to Exeter was constructed, the tiny settlement became isolated and later abandoned. It is said that the church was still in use as late as 1857. In the 1880s, efforts were made to try to preserve what little then remained of the old church. The oak screen was rescued and adapted to fit across the chancel of the 'new' St. Gabriel's church, built in 1840, in the nearby village of Morcombelake. The hillside which would once have been the churchyard for the old village, gives no hint of memorials to show where it once lay. It has been left to sink back into the earth; for the old inhabitants used to say that if any attempt were made to plough the land, the ploughshare would shatter, as holy ground could not be ploughed. It was also said that in the early part of the 19th century the chapel was use by smugglers as a storage place for smuggled casks of brandy.

The legend which tells the sad story of

A Tragic Tale of Shipwreck, Love and a Miracle

Bertram and his bride was probably written in the last two hundred years, but the author is unknown. It is a melodramatic tale of a shipwreck off this treacherous coast. Only the brave Bertram and his lovely bride escaped when the tall ship went down, and they were tossed on the rough waves for several days in their tiny boat. Bertram prayed continuously to St. Gabriel and promised that if their lives were saved, he would build a chapel to the saint. When the little boat was finally cast ashore the bride was already dead and Bertram was broken-hearted. He prayed again to St Gabriel for help to keep his vow, and suddenly crowds of people came running from every direction, although the place was virtually uninhabited. The huge crowd set to work, quarrying and carrying stone, and in no time a small chapel had been built to the honour of St Gabriel. Inside the chapel, they raised an altar, and reverently buried the beautiful lady beneath it. Then as if in memory of her golden hair they lit a glowing lamp to serve as a landmark for sailors. The last verse of the legend runs ....

> "Another chapel to this day
> Braves the rough storm wind well,
> And proves the vow fulfill'd, I trow,
> To good St. Gabriel."

No-one knows who Bertram was, or what ship he sailed in, or whether the stone from the building of the chapel was really quarried nearby. Nor is the period of history known. Today the ruins of the little chapel still stand, and the sunken lane still leads down to the sea. The view is breathtaking if you stand by the ruined chapel and gaze towards Lyme Regis. When the wind rises and a storm begins to blow — then you begin to appreciate how desolate this place must have been when poor Bertram carried his dying bride from the tiny wrecked boat.

A storm-tossed ship off the Dorset coast

The ruins of St. Gabriel's Church

49

Monks v Townspeople

"The towne has suffered from vyces, Idelnes, and unlawfull games by reson of so grete and inordynat nomber of Alehouses, in tyme of plentifulness, by Journeymen, day labourers and other poor Artyfycers there and thyder resorting and usying there ryotous expenses and unlawfull games to the grete trouble and inquyetyng of the inhabitaunts next thereto adjoynyng and to the grete Inpouerysshyng and decay of the Towne".

Certainly Sherborne had an 'inordinate number' of alehouses as did Shaftesbury and many other Dorset towns, but whether the townspeople quite deserved the accusations laid down in the above deed, which was drawn up in the 21st year of the reign of Henry VIII, is open to question. One suspects that they were no better and no worse than the inhabitants of any other town, even if they were given to "outbreaks of light-heartedness" as Treves so charmingly puts it.

Sherborne was known for a number of things, not just for its numerous taverns, but for its 'church-ales', for the processions and plays it staged on Corpus Christi Day in June, for its Market and for the great Pack Monday Fair. Then as now, the beautiful Abbey dominated the town, which was almost entirely built of golden Ham Hill stone. Charming narrow streets and alleyways, raised walkways and shady paths gave the old town an air of quiet and serenity which characterises it still. The name 'Sherborne' is derived from the Saxon 'Scir-burne', (clear stream) for the town stands on the River Yeo.

Charles Leland liked it too, for he wrote...

'The towne of Sherborne standith partly on the brow of a hill partly in a botom. I esteme it to lak little of a two miles in cumpace. For a dry town or other, saving Pole (Poole) that is a little thing, I take it to be the best towne at this present tyme in Dorsetshire."

Sherborne is still a charming town with many beautiful old buildings, many of them connected with the Abbey. In the Abbey close are the 14th century almshouses, whose outer appearance shows little change for the passage of 500 years. The Abbey was founded in 705 AD, in the reign of King Ine, the Wessex King who did so much to further the cause of Christianity in his kingdom. The first Bishop was the great St Aldhelm, for the see had been divided into two with Winchester as the centre of the Eastern side and Sherborne for the area to the West of the Selwood Forest. The great school was founded at the same time, and the scholarly traditions of the town have passed down in an unbroken line for 12 centuries.

As in most Abbey towns, the people of the town were allowed to use the nave of the Abbey as their Parish Church, for they had no other to use. But as the town grew in size, this was no longer adequate for their needs, so in the 14th century All Hallows Church was built, directly abutting the West end of the Abbey. The monks responded by almost blocking up the great West door, leaving only a narrow entrance into All Hallows. This would not have mattered except for the fact that the church had no font of its own, so the people were still compelled to use the font in the Abbey. This was now extremely difficult because of the

A Violent Quarrel in Sherborne Abbey

narrow entrance. So the townspeople decided to put up their own font.

The monks took strong objection to this — feeling that their priestly function was being compromised. There were angry words on both sides. The townspeople, feeling spiteful, took to ringing their new church bells at all hours of the night to annoy the monks. This was the last straw, and relations became so strained between the two parties that in 1436 the Bishop decided to hold an inquiry. The inquiry made several important decisions, namely that the All Hallows font should be destroyed and the West doorway of the Abbey widened again to give access to the Abbey font, and that the people should not ring their bells at unsuitable times. Neither side agreed with the decisions taken by the inquiry and things went from bad to worse. The monks, who were not quite as holy as they might have been, persuaded one Walter Gallor, a "stoute Bocher" dwelling in Sherborne, to enter All Hallows, where he "defacid clene the Fontstone". That did it, and what happened next is related in full by Leland ....

> "The townsmen, aided by an Erle of Huntindune lying in those quarters, rose in playne sedition ... A Prest of Alhalowes shot a shaft with fier into the Toppe of that part of S. Marve Chirch (the Abbey) that divided the Est part that the monks usid from that the Townes-men usid; and this partition chauncing at that Tyme to be thakked yn the Rofe was sette a fier and consequently al the hole chirch, the Lede and Belles meltid, was defacid".

The walls of the choir in the Abbey bear red marks to this day, scars of that bitter feud.

The only solution was to allow the people's own church, All Hallows, to be used without restraint or interference from the monks. The doorway however remained narrow as can be seen to this day.

"Retribution", Treves comments, "long after fell upon the monks", for the Abbey was dissolved in 1539 along with all the other great religious houses of Dorset. In the following year the building and grounds passed to Sir John Horsey of Clifton Maybank, who promptly re-sold the whole property to the people of Sherborne for the princely sum of £300. Treves comments ...

> "Thus were the tables turned upon the narrow-minded and selfish people of the monastery".

All Hallows Church was immediately pulled down as the congregation now had a much finer place in which to worship.

So the great Abbey still stands, a chequered history behind it, having narrowly escaped destruction on a number of occasions. The beauty of the stonework lives on, perpetuating the skills of the masons who shaped it and the artists who designed it.

The West end of the Abbey, showing the small door, and the remains of an arch of Allhallows

The Court Leet

In Wareham, on certain evenings in November, a number of quaintly dressed men, some in top hats, some in Dorset smocks, can be seen entering one pub after another. Once inside, they peer up the chimney, weigh loaves of bread on old-fashioned scales, taste the ale and levy a fine on the landlord if the service is not to their liking. These are the Officers of Wareham's Court Leet, which is a present-day survival of an ancient local court which existed long before local Government as we know it had even been invented.

Courts Leet were once held in most towns and villages, presided over by the Lord of the Manor or his steward. These courts dealt exclusively with local matters and carried out similar roles to those of today's Health and Safety Executive, Fire Prevention Officers and Trading Standards Departments. In some places there were other specifically local concerns as well, and often minor criminal or civil offences were dealt with, for the visits of Crown Judges were often few and far between.

Most of the Dorset Court Leet ceremonies seem to have died out in the early years of this century, but in one or two places, notably Portland and Wareham, the old customs are still kept up even though their officers today have no real power, for Town Councils and County Councils fulfil those functions.

At Winterborne Anderson up to 1905 or 1906, the Court Leet was held in the Manor House around the time of Martinmas (11th November). The Town Crier would go round with his bell to inform the local people when the court was to take place. After the court sitting, the Lord of the Manor would visit all his cottages to check for repairs. At Silton the court was held under a huge old oak tree, while at Corfe Mullen it was held at the *Cock and Wheatsheaf.* Here, it took place several times after 1918, but later died out. The officers of the Court met once a year. First the Agent of the Canford Estate sent for the Foreman of the Jury, who then summoned the other eleven Jurymen. They were paid 8 shillings for attending. Their main duty was to ensure maintenance of the water courses in the village, and to make sure that stray cattle were impounded.

At Sturminster Newton the following Officers were appointed, a Town Crier, a 'Chimney-peeper' who reported dirty chimneys, a 'Hayward' who took charge of straying cattle for which he received 4d each, and a 'Pounder' who put the cattle in the pound and looked after them. He received 2d each time he turned the key. Unfortunately he had to feed the cattle while they were impounded, so was often out of pocket, and found it more convenient and cheaper to ignore the straying cattle!

At Portland the Court Leet took place twice a year, and perpetuated several ancient arrangements dating back to Saxon times. As well as collecting rents the Court Leet administered royalties paid by the quarrymen on the stone taken out of the ground. The royalty of 1 shilling a ton was always paid half to the King, and half to the tenants, but in 1665, Charles II made a grant of 3d per ton from his half of the money to reward the Portlanders for their loyalty during the Civil War. This arrangement still stands, and the money thus collected goes into a public fund for the benefit of the people of Portland.

Collecting liquid 'fines' in the communal pot

Ancient Local Government Customs

Wareham Court Leet still survives in almost its complete original state, as far as we know. It takes place in November and has Officers designated as follows ...'Ale-Tasters', 'Bread-weighers', 'Flesh and Fish-tasters' (carnisters) 'Overseers of pavements' and 'Chimney-peepers'. There is a Bailiff-Steward and a Jury of twelve. There are also two 'Constables' and a couple of 'Scavengers', whose instructions from the Bailiff read as follows ....

"Ye shall see that the streets, lanes, privies, closets and cesspits are clean and in good order, and report to the Court"

The Lord of the Manor who is responsible for convening the annual Court is James Ryder of Rempstone, while the present Bailiff, of many years standing, is Herbert Elmes. Mr Elmes is now eighty-four years old and would like to retire, but his attempts to do so have been 'blocked' by the Court, who say that he must give ten years' notice! One of the main duties of the Court Leet used to be the overseeing of grazing rights. The need for this has all but disappeared and the activities are now confined to visiting all the pubs in the town, ostensibly to weigh their bread, taste their beer, and inspect the chimneys and the toilets. It is clearly an occasion of much fun and frivolity, for the landlords tend to bake outrageous sizes and shapes of bread, which won't fit on the scales, and the system of fines is so arbitrary that they get fined if they are within the regulations, and fined if they are not. If toilets are in a bad state, the team is just as likely to smash the toilets up with sledgehammers, after awarding the 'golden ballcock' for the worst toilets, though to be fair, they always rebuild what they have knocked down. Bystanders who misbehave when the constables are about their duties are quite likely to get handcuffed to the nearest fixture and left there!

On the Friday of Court Leet week, the Court sits in the Town Hall to hear the reports of the week's activities, and also to discuss other local questions, such as damage to the town walls which was discussed at the meeting of 1988. At the same meeting there was discussion of the new bypass and the problem of stray supermarket trolleys.

The whole affair is very light-hearted today, and during the week of visits a certain amount of alcohol is consumed as the team of peepers and inspectors and tasters visit eight pubs. Instant fines are levied on the landlord if any faults are uncovered. The fines take the form of tots of whisky which are poured into a large pot said to have been saved from the last Great Fire, 200 years ago.

So, in this charming little town, said to have a history which is "one long lurid tale of disaster and woe", the townspeople obviously still have a sense of humour as well as a keen interest in keeping alive a 900 year-old tradition.

The 'Chimney Peepers' in action

Some Dorset Trees

The long avenue of beech trees by Badbury Rings

After the Great Fire of Blandford in 1731, two families lived inside the hollow trunk of the giant Damory Oak, just north of where The Damory Oak Inn, on Damory Court Street, Blandford, now stands. The present inn sign shows children playing round the tree, which was said in Cromwell's time to have measured 68 feet in circumference, with room for 20 men inside. During the Civil War an old man is said to have used the tree as a booth for selling ale. The name Damory shows the local connection with the D'Amorie estate and Damory Court, once the property of the well-known Ryves family of Blandford. In 1755, the huge tree was felled and chopped up for firewood, raising £14 in the process.

Our pagan forefathers made sacrifices to the spirits who lived in the trees. Sacred groves were set apart for ritual and ceremony. Many surviving remnants of such ancient beliefs are to be found in our folklore, where certain trees and their attendant legends have passed down in folk memory. In Dorset, as in most other counties, there are a fair number of trees which have significance in this way.

Tree superstitions are common everywhere, but Dorset has a few of its own. For instance, the dense yew forest which once grew on Hambledon Hill, near Shillingstone, was said to have been planted by the Devil as his version of a sacred grove. This eerie place was long thought to be evil and 'unlucky'.

Treves mentions 'Soldier's Clump' on the edge of the wood opposite The Knoll in the older part of Corfe Mullen. Tradition says that many soldiers lie buried there, though of what army no-one knows. The legend states that they died at Badbury Rings. Not surprisingly, the area is said to be haunted by the ghosts of the soldiers.

The most well-known tree in Dorset must surely be the Monmouth Ash, off the Horton Road near Woodlands, in what was once a bleak and desolate area. Monmouth hid here, in a nearby ditch and was later captured and taken to Ringwood, a few miles down the road, before being taken to London to meet his fate. At Tolpuddle, the tree under which the six Tolpuddle martyrs met to discuss their plans for a union was thought to have died, but its rotten trunk is now sprouting branches again. A plaque relates its history.

At Woodlands on the corner of the road leading to Horton stands the 'Remedy Oak'. Here King Edward VI healed people of the 'King's Evil' or scrofula. In those days the King was believed to have a 'divine touch' and contemporary reports mention several monarchs who had this gift. The legend under the massive hollow oak reads ... "According to tradition King Edward VI sat under this tree and 'touched' for the King's Evil."

In former times, a person who committed suicide was denied a Christian burial and would often be buried at crossroads. The significance of the crossroads being that if the unhappy ghost should try to return, it would lose its way. When such a burial took place a nearby tree was often marked with a cross which acted as a marker for the spot. One Dorset tree bears a coffin-shaped mark, which marks the grave of a dairymaid who hanged herself around the end of the 18th century. A gate nearby is called 'Maiden's Grave Gate'. The 'Coffin Tree' as it is known, and the gate are in West Purbeck, on the boundary be-

The Remedy Oak near Woodlands

Living Landmarks and Legends

tween two parishes, not far from Baltington Farm, near Tyneham, where the unfortunate girl is said to have lived.

At Badbury Rings there is a beautiful avenue of stately beech trees, some 365 in number, though local folk say they cannot be counted accurately. They were planted in 1835 by the Kingston Lacy Estate, and in the fierce storms of winter 1990 several dozen were felled by the strong winds.   A re-planting programme is underway, to try to restore the avenue to its former glory.

There is a unique representation of a tree in the church of Gussage St Andrew, down the lane beside Chapel Farm. Here is depicted the only known representation in this country of Judas hanging from a tree. The traditional legend states that in his remorse after the Crucifixion, he hung himself from an elder tree. The form of the trunk shown in these barely visible remnants of medieval wall-paintings certainly looks as if it could have been an elder, but the branches are not visible.

Treves describes the pretty village of Fontmell Magna in his usual lyric fashion, mentioning the 'Gossip's Tree' as the focus of village togetherness. .....

> "Following the main road, one soon comes to the beautiful village of Fontmell Magna, which still boasts of a Maypole. It lies in a hollow by the side of the Fontmell Brook, and is as pretty a spot as old cottages, old gardens, and old orchards can make it. In the centre of the village is a very ancient tree with seats round it, where the gossips of the place congregate to mumble over flocks and herds, and the affairs of pigs."

'Culliver's Tree' is not a tree at all. It is a place, near Nottington between Dorchester and Weymouth. It was once part of the 'hundred of Culvard' — that is to say, 'Culvard's terrae' or lands. Treves said that a careless scribe turned Culvard into 'Culliver' and 'terrae' into tree, and that this anomaly was never corrected.

Cranborne Chase was once an extensive forest, upon which many people depended for their livelihood, the old woodland crafts of coppicing, charcoal burning and the making of thatching spars and hurdles being intensively followed until the end of the last century. In the hunting season, whole families actually lived in the woods to make sure of collecting a good harvest of nuts. Later, others moved in for the holy crop. the forest was indeed a busy place and a very important part of the rural economy. The Chase was also famous as a hunting-ground, and of course for its gangs of poachers. Hardy's description reflects on the great age of the woodlands ...

> "A truly venerable tract of forest land, one of the few remaining woodlands in England of uncounted primeval date, wherein druidical mistletoe is still found on aged oak, and where enormous yew trees, not planted by the hand of Man, grow as they had grown when they were pollarded for bows."

Pollarding was once very extensive in woodland management. The tree trunk is cut at a height of 8 to 20 feet above the ground which encourages the growth of new branches all from this one 'crown', producing a ready supply of timber poles, where coppicing is difficult because of grazing animals.

Old Country Games and Sports

In 1576, the Archbishop of York asked all his clergy whether they had allowed any ..."lords of misrule, or summer lords and ladies, or any disguised person, in Christmas or may games, or any Morris dancers ...etc" — for the Puritan ideal was to replace all such frivolities with preaching and sermons. The Puritans had already banned mystery plays and religious processions, broken up the guilds and fraternities and also sought to ban all church 'ales' and parish revels.

From the earliest times English people have certainly known how to enjoy themselves. Dorset has many records which show how people in earlier times "let their hair down". Two or three hundred years ago people did not have annual holidays as such, but they did celebrate a great number of 'high days and holidays' throughout the year. Many of the celebrations actually took place in and around the churchyard, which understandably caused some friction. From time to time, even before the Puritan era, the authorities did try to stamp out the more rowdy games — as early as 1311 the Bishop ordered that rough games in the churchyard at Shaftesbury would have to stop, while in 1477 Bishop Latimer complained that 'other sports' kept the young men from the archery butts and their practice. The other sports at that time would have included handball, tennis, football, hockey, dice, quoits, bowls, skittles and cock-fighting — though many of these would have borne little resemblance to their modern counterparts.

Not all games took place in churchyards, there was always the village green, and often local hilltops or earthworks were the site of fairs and feasts. Typically the gatherings tended towards the rowdy, and there was frequent trouble and drunkenness, as one might expect when healthy country folk decided to exert themselves in the sort of activities one thinks of nowadays in connection with 'It's a Knock-out' on television. The number and variety of the games played is astonishing, as can be seen by the wording of a handbill put out to advertise a country sports held on Maiden Castle, in the presence of King George III and a large Royal party, on September 29th 1789 ...

> "... to be played for at cricket — a round of beef, each man of the winning set to have a ribband; a cheese to be rolled down the hill — prize to whoever stops it; a silver cup to be run for by ponies, the best of three heats; a pound of tobacco to be grinned for; a barrel of beer to be rolled down the hill — prize to whoever stops it; a Michaelmas goose to be dived for; a good hat to be cudgelled for; half a guinea for the best ass, in three heats; a handsome hat for the boy most expert in catching a roll dipped in treacle and suspended by a string; a leg of mutton and a gallon of porter to the winner of a race of hundred yards in sacks; a good hat to be wrestled for; half a guinea to the rider of the ass who wins the best of three heats, by coming in last; a pig-prize to whoever catches him by the tail ..."

Clearly a great time was had by all.

The most popular sports among the younger country men and lads were, in Dorset, and in the neighbouring counties of Somerset and Wiltshire, 'Single-stick' or cudgel-playing, also known as 'back-swording', 'cut-leg', and the game of Fives,

An early version of rounders perhaps?

Cudgel-playing, Cut-leg and Grinning

described elsewhere. Single-stick was played with cudgels, usually a hazel stick, about three feet long and an inch in diameter, often with a hand-guard made of wicker. The two protagonists, in shirtsleeves, had one hand tied behind their backs. They played on a platform and the object was to make the opponent bend double, using blows to the body between the neck and knees. As soon as one bent, he could be whacked over the head with the stick. When blood was drawn, and if it ran for an inch, the cry went up, "One head broken — another man needed," and another challenger would step forward. There was a keen following for the game especially in the villages around Sherborne, Pulham, Caundle, Holnest and Hermitage, as well as in Sherborne itself. According to Hone's *Everyday Book* there were some inter-county championships with teams of up to 20 men.

'Cut-leg' was played with a similar weapon, but this time the object was to strike the opponent behind the knees — whoever could stand the longest being the winner.

Unfortunately cruel sports were for centuries very much part of the local scene. Cock-fighting was exceedingly popular among all classes of people. It was banned in 1795, but certainly continued secretly long after this date. Bull and bear-baiting were also much enjoyed from as early as the 12th Century. The spectacle of bulls, bears and also badgers being tormented by specially brutalised, mastiff-type dogs was a popular one worldwide. In this country all these cruel sports were banned by Parliament in 1835 when it was forbidden to keep a pit or house for the baiting or fighting of bulls, bears, dogs or any other animals. Badger-baiting survived much longer. Just over the border with Somerset, in the picturesque village of East Coker, badger hunts were organised in the 1920s by another of my uncles, who was the landlord of the *Helyar Arms*.

Many of the more harmless games survived well into the 20th Century and their natural successors, the Donkey Derby and the rustic 'welly-whanging' contests are still enjoyed today by Dorset folk.

Miracles in Dorset

The quietest woman in Dorset must surely be the one who carries her head beneath her arm! She is depicted on the inn sign of *The Quiet Woman* at Halstock, near the Somerset border. The legend is an ancient one, and one which follows a common theme in saintlore — for she was a 7th century saint named Juthware or Judith, who used to help pilgrims on their way to Halstock. Her jealous step-mother and her son resented her friendship with strangers, and the son attacked Juthwara one day, cutting off her head with his sword. Like many other saints she suffered this ignoble fate with fortitude. Juthwara calmly picked up her head and carried it to the church before dying. Needless to say, her ghost is said to haunt the lane at Judith Hill where the murder took place.

Miracles were apparently fairly common in medieval times in Dorset, as elsewhere, they were a strong attraction to pilgrims who brought money to the religious houses and fame to the shrines they visited. One of Dorset's best-known saints was Edward the Martyr, the young King who was cruelly murdered at Corfe by his step-mother and her henchmen, on March 18th AD 987. This horrific deed shocked the nation, and it is small wonder that many tales grew up around the events at that time. After the murder it was said that Edward's body was taken to the nearby cottage of an old blind woman. Inadvertently she touched the corpse, and immediately her sight was miraculously restored. The first thing she saw was a bush of white broom in full flower. She made a vow that she would place a sprig of this broom on his grave each year. The young King's body as taken to Shaftesbury Abbey for burial on the 20th February the following year, in a great state procession with noblemen and eminent churchmen. The old woman was true to her word and made the pilgrimage from Corfe each year thereafter. All along her route the white broom sprang up and flowered, becoming known as 'Martyr's Broom', or 'Martha's Broom'.

The fame of Edward's tomb soon spread, as Treves comments ...

> "Miraculous cures were wrought at the martyr's tomb, and such grace was with it, that the sick, the sad and the penitent came from all parts of the land to the sanctuary to seek peace."

A further legend tells how Edward's body came to be moved from the tomb to a special shrine within the Abbey Church, stating that on the 20th June 1001, when the remains had been in the grave for 22 years, the cover was miraculously lifted and a sweet odour was emitted. (Many stories of saints have this thread running through them — that the saint's remains were uncorrupted after many years in the grave). This lifting of the lid was taken to mean that Edward was dissatisfied with his resting place. At the time of this translation, the jaw bone and other parts of the remains were dispersed to other religious houses at Durham, Abingdon, Salisbury and elsewhere, for every piece of the saint's body held part of its miraculous power. For many years the streets of Shaftesbury were crowded with pilgrims making their way to the Abbey gates. The remains of Edward were believed lost, until 1931 when a rough lead casket was uncovered containing part of the skeleton of a young man. The Abbey ruins were privately owned, and the owner later bequeathed the casket to a branch of the Russian

St. Wite's shrine, Whitchurch Canonicorum Church

Orthodox Church. A long legal wrangle is still going on, for the people of Shaftesbury believe that the rightful place for these remains is in the gently crumbling ruin which is all that now remains of Shaftesbury Abbey.

Another very well-known shrine is that of St Wite or St Candida at Whitchurch Canonicorum. Here under a stone slab the bones of a very small woman were found in a damaged casket in 1900. Beneath the slab is the 13th Century shrine, with three large holes where sick people could place their diseased limbs while praying to the saint to restore them to health. The history of St Wite is very obscure, and the speculations of many historians have pointed to the theory that she was a saint from Brittany, also known as Blanche. St Wite's holy well can also be seen, on the side of Chardown Hill at Morcombelake. Here those suffering from eye complaints would bathe their eyes and pray for a cure.

Proof that miracles are still happening in Dorset is shown by a story from Hilfield, near Cerne Abbas. This remote place is home to a modern-day order of Friars, the Society of St Francis, founded in 1931, as an Anglican order, which now has branches worldwide. At Hilfield, the Brothers run a hostel for 'wayfaring men' and also care for others who need a home and support. The oldest

St. Edward the Martyr's Shrine, Shaftesbury Abbey

member of the community, Brother Kenneth, remembers a time when they had no money at all, and things looked very bleak. The only course left open to them was to pray — and by the next post came a package containing £100 in £1 notes.

59

Buried Treasure

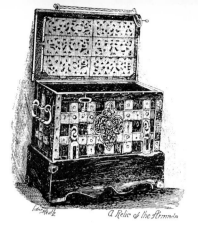

Treasure chest

A coffin of solid gold lies buried at Milborne St Andrew, and if any person should try to dig for it — there will be instant retribution in the form of a violent storm with thunder and lightning, to deter them from their task!

Local legends like this are very common in Dorset as elsewhere and serve to protect the supposed treasure from gold-seekers who might cause problems. Gold has always had an air of mystery attached to it and legends like this usually suggest that some harm will come to those who seek the treasure and often that the hoard is guarded by ghosts, or even by demons, to keep people away. To go off and seek for treasure was always a hazardous undertaking, as we see in so many folk tales and fairy stories.

Many of Dorset's hidden treasure stories are linked with ancient earthworks or burial mounds, perhaps because in the past many have been opened and found to contain valuable artefacts. Another golden coffin is said to be under a barrow called 'Warbarrow' or 'Playbarrow' at Sixpenny Handley, though apparently Pitt-Rivers did not find it when he excavated the site. Treasure is also said to be buried under the burial mounds along the Bere Regis to Wimborne Road.

At Badbury Rings, as Treves tells us there is yet another coffin buried ....

> ".... on the grassy summit of an open down, the only object in a windswept solitude. ..... founded by the Celts and added to by the Romans and Saxons. ..... Somewhere under the cap of pines and oaks, or beneath the wave-like rings of entrenchments, there lies buried a coffin of solid gold, still bright and wonderful"

He also refers to the tradition that Badbury Rings is the 'Mount Badon' of legend, where King Arthur defeated the West Saxons, which adds the mystery of the 'once and future King' to the many other mystical connections of this place.

At Tarrant Gunville, there is a legend of a silver coffin which, it is said, lies buried under some yew trees just outside the village. The table buried on the site of the 14th Century Sturminster Castle, of which nothing now remains, is made of gold. Again there is a link with King Arthur, for it is said to be a replica in miniature of the famous Round Table, and that it was once kept in the castle. The legend states that it was removed and thrown down a well, perhaps for safe keeping, but no one has yet managed to find a well on the site.

A legend of Winterborne Kingston tells that a King lies buried in a gold coffin. When some local labourers dug up what they thought was the precious coffin, it is said to have crumbled away before their eyes. This event took place at the end of the last century, it may not have put the story to rest, for such legends have a way of continuing for many years in local memory.

There is a long tradition of hidden treasure at Shaftesbury Abbey, although repeated excavations have so far failed to find it, apart from a few trinkets of gold wire found with buried corpses. The story goes that when the Dissolution of the abbey was imminent, the Abbess gave one of the monks a casket of treasure to hide. This he did, but unfortunately died of a stroke before he could tell the Abbess where he had hidden it. Is it this same monk whose ghostly form has often been seen walking the pathways among the ruins — perhaps looking for the Abbess to tell her his

Woodbury Hill, a golden table is said to be hidden in the Anchoret's Well, but the well cannot be found

secret?

There are, however, a few Dorset stories of actual treasure being found. A jet and gold sceptre-head was found in Clandon Barrow near Martinstown during excavations, and near Milton Abbey about a hundred years ago a 50-inch long wreath of gold was found together with a gold ring. These were thought to be about 2000 years old. At Loders, an earthen pot containing hundreds of silver coins was found. Probably the hoard of some Tudor miser.

An undated story from Ansty tells how some labourers were draining a meadow when they came across a golden chaplet with two trumpet-shaped ornaments at the tip and with it a gold armlet. This was said to be 'treasure-trove', and was once in the keeping of the Earl of Port Arlington.

In Lyme Regis in 1786, a labourer named George Kelway was infilling an old saw-pit which had been dug amongst the ruins of an old house — when he found three old chests containing immense quantities of gold and silver coin of the reign of Charles I and II, amounting to more than £2000, a considerable sum of money at that time. It is supposed that the chests were probably buried at about the time of Monmouth's adventure in 1685.

George Kelway loaded himself up with as much as he could carry, then hurried home. He told his landlord, who went back with him and they began to gather another load. Unfortunately they dropped some and very soon the whole neighbourhood knew, all the townspeople came rushing to fill their pockets and caps, literally 'rolling in money' as the source puts it. Kelway and his helper got away with about 140lb of gold and silver. Sadly the landlord was soon tricked out of most of it by a crafty tinker while Kelway was absent. The tinker called Roe, was caught and imprisoned, and most of the money was recovered.

As may be expected Dorset's coastline has witnessed a number of incidents in which the citizens have taken advantage of a shipwreck to enrich themselves, some of which, to say the least, have been rather shameful. One such incident was the wreck of the *Hope of Amsterdam* on the Chesil Bank in 1748, when a cargo of gold worth £50,000 was cast up on the shore. Reports say the beach "was held by the mob for ten days", and that the people scrabbled and fought over the treasure.

On other occasions lost cargoes of fine spirits have been responsible for rendering the local inhabitants very cheerful!

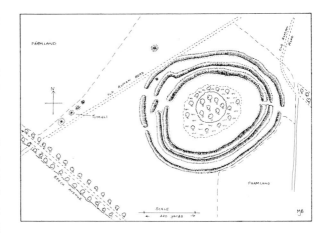

Badbury Rings, focus of many mysterious legends

Easter Celebrations

Bread baked on Good Friday never goes mouldy — in fact, if kept, it will act as a charm and will prevent all other bread baked in the house from going mouldy! Similar qualities were attributed to Hot Cross buns baked on the same holy day. Indeed, Good Friday buns were often kept and used for healing purposes — for a small piece soaked in water was considered to have curing properties for many ailments, and was especially good for any kind of cattle disease. The sign of the cross on the buns is said to stem from an old belief that the cross would prevent witches from dancing over the dough when it was laid aside to prove. The buns themselves have their origins in the dim and distant past, for they are believed to derive from the small cakes made for the Celtic festival of Spring. This is a good example of the 'holy' intermixing with the 'magical' whereby pagan practices are 'Christianised' only superficially and retain their 'magical' characteristics in the minds of people.

Easter was the most important festival of the Christian year, symbolising as it does the Redemption of Man and the confirmation of the fundamental belief in Life Everlasting. For country folk it meant a holiday, several holidays in fact and as one would expect, the people took full advantage of the season. It was also the beginning of spring and many of the older spring ceremonies inevitably became muddled with Christian festivities. Holy Week began with Palm Sunday when expeditions went off to find sallow in the woods, for Palm-Sunday crosses. In neighbouring Wiltshire, there was always a fair on top of Silbury Hill and figgy-cakes were the dish of the day. At Cheselbourne in Dorset, girls dressed in white would walk in the fields, 'treading in the wheat', which was certainly a survival of some ancient type of fertility rite.

Good Friday was a holy day when the Devil was powerless, especially between the hours of noon and 3 pm, about the time of the Crucifixion. Very widespread among country folk everywhere was the idea that Good Friday planting was 'blessed', an idea that still persists to this day, for many will still be sure to plant their potatoes on Good Friday. Anything sown, planted or transplanted on that day will do well. Flowers will 'come double' if sown on Good Friday and it is an auspicious day for all crops, especially parsley. Indeed if it is planted on any other day it is probable that nothing will come up at all. The plant is notoriously slow to germinate — this is said to be because it belongs to the Devil and it has to go down seven times to its master before it can come up!

There used to be many taboos about Good Friday. No iron tools or nails should be used because of the evil use they were put to on the first Good Friday, consequently no blacksmith would work. No fishermen would put to sea and miners would not go underground. It was also said to be taboo to throw away soapy water on Good Friday, or it would turn to blood. This appears to be connected to an old legend about a washerwoman who waved a wet garment at Jesus on his way to Calvary.

There are few customs or Easter traditions unique to Dorset, for Hot Cross buns are eaten everywhere, as were the flat white Easter cakes with currants, which are still eaten today. In some parts of the county 'skimmer cake' was traditional,

Gardening Magic
and Holy Buns

this was a kind of dough-cake boiled in a skimmer. The egg-rolling games which were so common in Northern counties were not known in Dorset, but eggs, coloured by boiling with onion skins or some other vegetable matter were given to the children, and there is some evidence of 'egg-shackling', where the hard-boiled eggs are rolled together in a seive — the last one to break is the winner. Eggs of course are a symbol of the Resurrection, and the religious symbolism of these rolling games is that the eggs represent the stone rolled away from Christ's tomb on Easter morning.

As everywhere, Easter Sunday was for parading at Church, in new clothes, especially bonnets, while Easter Monday was given over to the usual rustic sports and games. At Stalbridge there was a game called 'Crookern' which was played on the Ring. The first part of the game was called 'Hunting the Buck' when up to 50 men and women stood in a ring holding hands. One was chosen to be the 'Buck' and others adopted kneeling positions. It is not clear what happened after that, but the next stage was a kind of country dance, which ended up, not surprisingly, at the *Virginia Ash Inn* at Henstridge, where large quantities of beer were consumed. Udal comments that there are elements in this game which bear a resemblance to the Cornish 'Furry Dance'.

The Church was of course the focus for Easter celebration, particularly in pre-Reformation times when there were elaborate rituals including 'creeping to the cross'. A few Dorset churches still have an Easter sepulchre, which was a wide decorated niche, often on the North side of the altar. Here the sacred host was placed on Good Friday and watched over continuously till Easter Sunday when it was ceremoniously removed to the High Altar. There is one at Glanville's Wootton and another at Tarrant Hinton, which is inscribed in Latin, and can be translated as, "Come and see the place where the Lord lay". A black-draped cross was placed here on Good Friday, to be removed on Easter Day amid joyous hymn-singing. The Tarrant Hinton sepulchre was built in 1520, shortly before the Reformation put an end to such ceremonies. It is a particularly fine example, which would originally have been decorated with numerous figures and statues. St Peter's Church in Dorchester also had an Easter sepulchre with carved figures.

The Crucifixion, central to the Christian faith

Sea-Nymphs and Sirens

"Near the place where the famous Dee payeth his tribute to the German Ocean, curious observers of wonderful things in Nature will be please thither to resport the 1,13 and 29th May and on divers other times in the ensuing summer, as also in the harvest time, to the 7 and 14 October — they will undoubtedly see a pretty company of mar-maids, creatures of admirable beauty and likewise hear their charming sweet melodious voices."

This astonishing but entirely serious entry appears in Aberdeen's *New Prognostications for the Year 1688*. In those days people really believed in mermaids. For the Age of Exploration was still a wonder and explorers made good capital from the tales they brought back from far-off lands about strange people, animals and plants. As late as 1825, a so-called mermaid was being exhibited in a penny peep-show at Bartholomew Fair. *Chamber's Book of Days* however, described it as "a hideous combination of a dried monkey's head and body, and the tail of a fish, believed to have been manufactured on the coast of China."

Mermaid legends come down to us from very early times and from many parts of the world. Shakespeare knew them well and often mentions mermaids in his plays, as in Hamlet ...

"I'll drown more sailors than the mermaids shall."

Mermaid legends are as enduring as the age-old tales of sea-serpents and monsters, such as our own Loch Ness Monster, still sought by many. Traditionally, mermaids, like the 'Lorelei' of the Rhine, sat on the rocks enticing sailors to their doom. Their voices could enchant any man who heard them, who would then follow them wherever they led. The mermaids' wiles included tales of caskets of treasure and riches hidden in deep caverns and they would lull their captives into a trance-like sleep with their singing, luring them down, deep under the ocean, to dwell forever in a watery paradise. If a mermaid could marry a mortal man, she could lose her tail, and acquire legs. All sea-maidens had supernatural powers and could grant wishes or bestow curses if so minded.

Legend says that the town of Conway in Wales was cursed by a mermaid — for the people had refused to help her back in the water when she was cast ashore. She said there would be a fish famine and that the citizens of the town would always be poor. In Herefordshire there is a tale of a mermaid who guards a church bell which fell into the River Lugg, while the mermaid of Rostheren Mere may sometimes be heard ringing a church bell from deep under the water.

In the Orkneys, mermaids were the daughters of the Fin Folk who lived in a magical land under the sea, but they also farmed on the land. As they aged they became very ugly, which is why they always harboured a desire to become human, and avoid their fate. In the Fens, anyone who leaned too far over a pool was likely to be dragged into the water by a waiting mermaid. In Scotland in the 17th Century, two fishermen were said to have drawn up a mermaid with a hook. They described her as having "face, arms, breast, shoulders etc of a woman, and long hair hanging down her neck, but the nether-part from below the waist was hidden in the water". Unfortunately the fishermen lost her before they were able to examine her tail. A classic case of 'the one that got away'.

Beware the Song of the Mermaid

A mermaid captured in Greece in 1775 was said to be very beautiful with blue eyes and white teeth with fish-like gills for ears. She had a beautiful 'membrane' running from her temples like a headdress instead of the usual long golden hair. She had female breasts but no nipples, and no nails on her fingers. From the waist down she was like a cod-fish with three sets of fins. She was only three feet long including her tail, and was said to have an enchanting voice. It is not surprising to learn that this example too, was believed to be a fraud.

Cornwall, as one would expect, is rich in mermaid stories. The most famous one concerns the 'Mermaid of Zennor' who, disguised as a beautiful woman used to regularly attend services in the church. All the congregation were agog at her marvellous singing voice. Finally she tempted away the best tenor in the choir, who was never seen again. A representation of her was carved on an ancient bench end, now made into a chair, in Zennor church.

Dorset's most famous mermaid does not compare to her in beauty. Hutchins described her with what Treves calls 'scientific solemnity'. She was thrown ashore at Burton Bradstock in June 1757, and Hutchins says ...

"... This romantic individual, being no less than 13 feet in height or length, was evidently a giantess of the species. Her upper or better half had a human form, while her extremity was that of a fish. The head of this unhappy creature was partly like that of a man and partly like that of a hog. Her fins resembled hands. She had a masculine jawbone and 48 teeth in both the upper and the lower jaw".

There could of course be a logical explanation for Burton Bradstock's giant mermaid. The tropical 'sea-cow' manatee or dugong, which somewhat resembles a walrus, was often mistaken for a mermaid. Perhaps she was indeed a manatee washed up on our shores from South America by the Gulf Stream.

The fascination with mermaids is evidenced by the popularity of representations in churches. There is one in Whitcombe church, near Winterborne Came, and in Sherborne Abbey, high up among the fan-vaulting, is a beautiful coloured ceiling boss showing the legendary temptress, holding a comb and mirror in her hands.

The Mermaid of Zennor, Cornwall

Reeve-Poles at Portland

In October, 1834, the Houses of Parliament burnt down. The cause of the fire was the excessive heat generated by the stoves used to warm the chambers. The fuel consisted of quantities of the old 'Exchequer Tallies', which had been used in former times to keep the Manorial accounts. These continued to be used long after modern methods of accounting had been established.

In the reign of George II it was proposed that more up-to-date methods should now be adopted, but ...

> "All the red tape in the country grew redder, at the bare mention of this bold and original conception — and it took until 1826 to get these sticks abolished"

Hence it was decided to use them as fuel to keep their Lordships warm. The panelling in the Lords was soon well alight and the fire quickly spread to the Commons and eventually both houses were 'reduced to ash'.

But the old-fashioned methods were not abandoned everywhere. In Portland, a place well-known for its tendency to hang on to ancient custom long after the rest of the county — 'tally-sticks', or more correctly 'Reeve-staffs', were still in use in the early part of the 20th Century. Connected with their use was the old custom of 'Marrying the Land'. The only way that ownership of land could be transferred in Portland was by means of 'Church Gift'. The buyer and the seller both went to church and made a solemn declaration of the transaction, which was then considered legal and binding, for there were no paper records or deeds. The only records kept were in the form of easily recognisable notches on long staffs held by the Reeve, an official of the Court Leet.

Portland Court Leet was still an active authority at the beginning of this century, a Manorial Court dealing with the 'Rights, dues, Practices, and Customs of the Manor and with the Control and Management of the Commonable Lands.' Two courts were held every year, with 24 jurymen chosen from among the tenants. Portland was a Royal Manor and so the Lord in Chief was the King, who was represented by the steward of the manor. The Bailiff was responsible for summoning the Court, and the jurymen elected their own Foreman. Other officers were the Reeve, the Chief Constable, Inspectors, Affeerors (who fixed fines) and the Haywards, who protected the enclosed lands from straying cattle.

The Bailiff reported on the amounts of stone quarried from commonable lands, and also reported any deaths among the tenants, for 'half a crown' was payable to the Chief if a tenant died. The Constable and Inspectors were required to see that there were no encroachments on common lands and that roads and paths were preserved and also that there were no irregularities in the working of the quarries. In the case of encroachment a fine was levied.

All tenants of the Royal Manor were freeholders — quit rent being payable annually according to the notches on the Reeve-staff, marked up from entries in a rent-roll. The Reeve was appointed at the Michaelmas Court and held office for one year, during which time he is recompensed by the use of a piece of land called the 'Reeve-Plot'. No person was allowed to hold the office twice and it was usually held by the person paying the highest rents. A list showing all

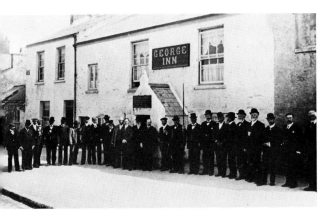

Portland Court Leet assembled with reeve-pole 1911

An old method of Accounting

the Reeves since 1700 includes the names of 14 women who have held the office.

The use of the Reeve-staff as a form of reckoning was invented far back in time when few could read or write. For many years the rent for an acre of land was fixed at 3d, payable to the chief, to a total of £14.14s. 3d. The rent of a cottage was a farthing and if it had a garden it was doubled to a halfpenny. The staff itself was made of deal, pine or mahogany, between 7 and 12 feet in length, and about 1½ inches square. Certain signs represented the five ancient hamlets of Portland; Southwell, Wakeham, Weston, Easton and Chiswell (Chesil). Long and short notches and lines represented the rent payable by each tenant according to the order in the Reeve Book. Individual amounts were separated by small dots or triangular cuts. The staff varied in length from year to year according to the number of tenants and the method of cutting. In later years simplified methods were introduced.

The first use of this type of accounting method in this country was recorded back in Saxon times, possibly brought here by Danish invaders. It is probably much older than that, for a similar type of stick is mentioned in the Old Testament, in Ezekiel-chapter 37 v 16, where marks were made on a stick to represent the tribes of Israel.

Reeve-staffs can be seen on display both at the Dorset County Museum in Dorchester and at the small Portland Museum.

Southwell	○
Wakeham	⊕
Weston	⊠
Easton	W
Chiswell	V

Paying 'Quit rent' at Portland

Early Christian Missionaries

Walpurgisnacht is the name given to the ancient Celtic Festival of Beltane on the night of 30th April/1st May. For witches it was the 'sabbat' second only in importance to Hallowe'en. This was a night for flying off on broomsticks, accompanied by evil spirits and ugly familiars — to while away the hours of darkness with their obnoxious celebrations. The venue was Brocken, the highest peak of the Harz Mountains in Germany, the gathering place of all the covens.

The link with Wimborne lies in the fact that a Wimborne nun of the 8th century, named Walburga, gave her name to the witches' festival. The name Walburga has many variations, both in Dorset and in Germany where she lived and worked for thirty-five years. She has been known as 'Valpurge', 'Gualbourg', 'Vaubone' and 'Avangour'. The Greek equivalent is 'Eucharis', which means 'gracious' or 'pleasing', fitting attributes for a great lady.

Walburga is an Anglo-Saxon name, for she was born in Devon. Her father was a West Saxon chief, King Richard. She had two brothers, St Winebald and St Willibald, and her uncle was the great St Boniface. It is easy to see that her whole background marked her out for a life of service and piety.

At that time, the building of the present Minister at Wimborne was many years off, but on the same site there was a convent dedicated to St Cuthberga. This had been established by two sisters, Cuthberga and Cwenburh, in the year 705. Walburga entered St Cuthberga's at an early age, and stayed there for twenty-seven years.

St Boniface, later martyred in Germany, who was Walburga's uncle, had been sent with Winebald and Willibald, his nephews, as missionaries to begin the task of converting the heathen races of Europe. He sent an appeal to Abbess Tetta of Wimborne to send him some nuns to help him in his work. Another relative, Boniface's cousin, Lioba, led the party of ten nuns which included Walburga. They undertook the hair-raising journey in a small boat, which scene was later represented by Rubens in a painting in the church of St Walburga in Antwerp. The same scene is also pictured in a fresco in the church of St Boniface in Munich.

The two brothers, Winebald and Willibald, had founded a monastery in Heidenheim, and Walburga was sent to be Abbess of the establishment, in support of the nuns. When her brother Winebald died in 760, she was appointed Abbess of the whole monastery by the Bishop of Eichstatt.

Walburga is always depicted wearing the robes of a Benedictine nun, carrying a staff and holding a flask of healing oil. The oil signifies her work, for she studied medicine and reportedly cured many poor people of various illnesses. She was loved and revered by all who knew her, for she led a blameless and pious life — with no hint of arrogance or pride in her bearing. It was said of her that she never expected others to do what she was unwilling to do herself. She and her party were the very first female English missionaries. St Cuthberga's, the forerunner of today's Minster, was therefore a great pioneering force in the strong tradition of English missionary work.

Walburga served in Germany for thirty-five years and died there in 779 AD, after a lifetime of devoted service. On May the 1st, 870 AD her

Walpurgisnacht and Wimborne

St Walburga and her companions on their way across the sea

remains were translated to Eichstatt to lie beside the body of her brother Winebald. This is probably why the existing pagan feast became known as 'Walpurgisnacht', perhaps originally in an attempt to 'Christianise' the celebration. After her burial, it was noticed that her bones exuded clear drops of liquid. Her devout followers attributed her healing powers to this 'oil' which was thereafter known as 'St Walburga's Oil'. Today, the saint's remains are enshrined in a magnificent tomb in the Abbey at Eichstatt, and the oil still exudes from her bones for five months a year, from October to February 25th, the anniversary of Walburga's death. This oil is reverently collected and bottled in tiny phials by the Benedictine nuns,

who send it all over the world to those who wish to benefit from St Walburga's influence. She is one of the world's most popular saints.

In 893 AD, in accordance with practice at the time, some of her relics were sent to other parts of Europe, which meant that her cult became more widespread, so that many churches all over Bavaria, Flanders and Burgundy were dedicated to her, perpetuating her name. She also figures in many German and Flemish religious paintings. Though her translation was May 1st, Walburga's actual feast day is the 25th of February.

As for the sisterhood of witches, the very name Walburga serves as protection against any evil they may perpetrate, at Beltane or any other time.

The present Minster is also dedicated to St. Cuthberga

The Evil Eye

"…. she could go through a key-hole, ride on a broomstick, turn herself into a hare, and run over to Chaldon and back before you could look round …"

This was the description of a West Lulworth woman condemned as a witch early in the 19th century. In fact she had been a very clever woman whose talents were suspected by the local people who thought she had help from the Devil. When she died her little dog sat by her grave refusing to move, which made the local folk all the more convinced that she was a witch!

Superstitious country folk were only too ready to believe in the existence of witches, wizards and the like. Dorset had a good share of the type of 'witch-hysteria' that swept other parts of the country, though there were apparently few really scandalous cases. Any old woman who lived alone, perhaps with a cat for company and who dabbled in the healing arts was liable to be called a witch. However ordinary folk needed such people — for a 'cunning-man' or 'white witch' was probably the only kind of medical treatment they could afford. But they were naturally fearful and when the prescription or treatment seemed a little out of the ordinary — then whispers would pass round about the strange abilities of the practitioner.

Such tales come from all parts of the county and are typified by the story of an old woman who lived at Spetisbury, who sat by the window all day long watching people go by. She was said to be able to stop an animal in its tracks by gazing at it with a fixed stare. The farmers were so much in fear of her that they supplied here with all the eggs

and cheese she could wish for! A similar witch was in action at Turner's Puddle, reported by a local man whose horse had refused to budge outside the witch's house. Two old ladies who lived at Sturminster Newton were called 'The Wormies', said to have the power of the 'Evil Eye' or 'overlooking'. They also used charms such as frog entrails in a little bottle and a bullock's heart stuck with pins. They in turn believed that the village schoolmaster was bewitching them and they scratched him with pins to break the spell. At Wyke Regis lived an old woman who, it was thought, had 'overlooked' a girl rendering her arm useless. The girl's mother was told how to counteract the spell by a gypsy, for gypsies were known to have a special knowledge of these things. The gypsy told the mother to hang up a bullock's heart stuffed with pins, inside the chimney. She did so and as the heart dried out, it fell into the fire and was burnt. The old woman was later seen tearing her hair in rage and screeching that someone had been meddling in her affairs. The same witch was said to have cursed a neighbour who later went bankrupt.

If pigs were unwell, the most obvious supposition was that they had been bewitched, and if the spell were countered by a charm they would recover. An example of this comes from East Stour where a Somerset wizard told the pigman to take hairs from the pig's back and burn them over a fire at midnight. The man did so and was very frightened by a loud bang on the door as he burnt the hair — the pigs began to recover the next day.

Occasionally horses would be found in their stables, sweating profusely and in a totally exhausted state — they were said to be 'hag-rid',

Witchcraft and Sorcery in Dorset

Two witches
'brewing up a storm'

referring to the belief that a witch had been riding the horses fast and furiously all night, returning them to their stable before dawn. Nine horses in the Cheselbourne area were said to have been killed in this way by 'Old Ann Riggs', a local witch. A similar story comes from Horton.

Not surprisingly, with such threatening possibilities in the air, simple country folk would try remedies suggested by the white witches to give themselves protection. A favourite method was a pig or bullock heart, stuck with pins or thorns and hung high up in the chimney, which was believed to spoil the witch's power. A number of these have been found in Dorset during building works on old houses. A great many small bottles have been found in similar circumstances, which usually contain some liquid substance. These were no doubt similar to the 'bottle charm' obtained by a Dorset man from a wizard in Yeovil, to counteract the evil spell cast on him by a neighbour. A horseshoe hung over the door was also a good protector and these can often be seen to this day over cottage doorways.

One belief about witches was very prevalent, this was the idea that they could turn themselves into hares. Such hares could appear and disappear at will and could never be caught. The only way to harm them was to shoot them with a bullet made from a silver sixpence. If the wounded hare really was a witch, then a local old woman would be found to have a cut on her back and so the witch would be revealed. Until her blood was drawn her mischief would not cease. Many tales of this nature came from the Purbeck area. Toads too, were handled with great respect in case they were the 'familiars' of the 'sly wold witch', as Barnes

would have called her. His poem 'A Witch', shows intimate knowledge of just what wickedness she could get up to ...

> "The dog got dead-alive and drowsy,
> The cat vell sick an' woulden mousey;
> An' every time the vo'k went up to bed,
> They were a-hag-rod till they were half dead.
> They us'd to keep her out o' house,'tis true,
> A-näilen up at door a hosses shoe;
> An' I've a-heärd the farmer's wife did try
> To dawk[1] a needle or a pin
> In drough her wold, hard wither'd skin,
> An' draw her blood, a-comèn by;
> But she could never vetch a drap,
> For pins would ply[2] an needles snap
> Ageän her skin; an' that in coo'se
> Did meäke the hag betwitch em woo'se.

[1] prick
[2] bend

The witch's workroom

The Whitsuntide Holiday

As long ago as 1570, the popular 'church-ale' at Blandford was being decried from the pulpit by William Kethe, as a day spent in "bullbeatings, berebeatings, bowling, dycing, carding, daunsynges, drunkenness, and whoredom, in so much as men could not keepe their servauntes from lyinge out of theyr owne houses the same Sabbath-day at night".

A not unfamiliar tale and one that was to be repeated many times over as the Puritans of the late 17th century tried to stamp out secular celebrations, particularly anything which gave rise to too much jollity on the part of ordinary people. Whitsun 'church-ales' were linked to the church, with the parish owning the equipment to prepare and serve food for large numbers of people. The better-off members of the community contributed to the feast which was for everyone in the parish. The churchwardens provided the ale and made all the arrangements and the event was usually held in a big barn near the church. Such events were also used to rise money for church repairs and other amenities and in spite of the reports of rowdy behaviour and disruption, the Bishop of Bath and Wells seemed to have been generally in favour, for in 1633, he reported as follows ...

> "I finde that by chuch-ales heretofore many poor Parishes have cast their Bells, repaired their Towers, beautified their Churches, and raised stocks for the poor."

Whitsuntide continued to be, for country folk, the most popular festival of all, combining as it did the village 'feast', parades and processions, called 'Club-walking', a church festival and a Spring festival all rolled into one. In the early years of this century such gatherings were still very popular in the villages and remained so right up to the 1920s. My mother and her sister, now both in their 80s, remember that the girls were always dressed in white for Whit-Sunday, with new hats and bright ribbons. There was considerable competition among the mothers to have the best turned-out daughters.

During the 19th century, these village feasts or revels tended to take the place of the old May day festivities, which had earlier died out. Every village had its 'Club' or 'Friendly Society', formed initially to collect and distribute funds for the purchase of family needs, emergency funds in time of sickness, or funeral expenses. In Marnhull, the 'Blue Club' or 'Friendly Society' was certainly in existence in the 1850s. The club met at first in a cart shed and later transferred to the *Crown Hotel*. The 'slate' or 'Loan Club' developed somewhat later. The feast day for Marnhull was held on the last Wednesday in May. The church bells rang early and folk gathered at the *Crown* with their ribbons and fairings for this greast village 'do'. First they processed to a service in the church and then the whole company paraded through the village, with banners, flags and garlands, going to every house for ale and cakes, with much jollity and dancing, along the way. Dinner was at the *Crown*, and this was followed by dancing, games and more drinking. These happy, community occasions, sadly died out in Marnhull during the last war.

'Club-walken' also took place at Symondsbury where a band accompanied the colourful procession, as it called round the houses for refreshments. A large marquee was set up for the feast and there were stalls and various entertainments.

Whit Tuesday Fair on the beach at West Bay, Bridport 1860

Club-Walking and Village Feasts

Stoke Abbot Club-walking continued until 1939, marching on the first Friday in June, with a brass band, silk banners and brass-topped staves. Once again a magnificent dinner was followed by dancing and amusements of the traditional kind. Garlands were carried in the procession at Lytchett Matravers, with a prize being given for the best one. The feast took place at the inn, and Maypole and country dancing carried on till late at night.

My uncle, Stan Bartlett, still lives in the village of Trent, where he was born 90 years ago. He can well remember 'Trent Feast', which took place in August, and also the 'Club-walking'. He told me how each club had a distinctive design for its brass-topped stave which was carried proudly in the procession, (Some of these can be seen in the Dorset County Museum). The Trent and Compton Friendly Society met on the first Tuesday of the month at the *Rose and Crown*. The club-walking day was Whit-Thursday. All the men wore white trousers and rosettes and the girls had new hats and white dresses. The band accompanied the parade, stopping off to see the squire and the parson on the way to the inn, where the feast would be waiting. Much beer was consumed on that day, and there was a skittle alley and coconut shies, among other amusements. Uncle Stan took part in what were the last few events of this kind in Trent, for the First World War came, when people had no heart for such things. Most of the Dorset clubs had died out by this time, due in part to new welfare and insurance arrangements.

It is sad that such picturesque and charming customs no longer take place. It is not hard to imagine the pleasure afforded to village children and young people by regular celebrations of this kind. William Barnes sums up the atmosphere for us perfectly ...

Whitsuntide an' Club-Walkèn

Zoo off they started, two an' two,
Wi' painted poles an' knots of blue,
An' girt silk flags, — I wish my box
'D a got em all in ceäpes and frocks, —
A-weäven wide an' flappèn loud
In playsome winds above the crowd;
While fifes did squeak an' drums did rumble,
An' deep beäzzoons did grunt an' grumble,
An' all the vo'k in gathrèn crowds ..."

A typical Whit Sunday scene, before the procession, about 1900

The Silver Well

An evil face with a smoke-hole, Cerne Abbas Church

St Augustine struck his staff into the ground and 'fetched out a crystal fountain, saying "Cerno deum" (I see God)'. So runs the legend concerning the visit of St. Augustine to Dorset. Augustine arrived in Kent in 597 AD on a mission from Rome to bring Christianity to this heathen land. It is not known if he actually came to Dorset but for a village to have a 'holy' well was something quite special so it was customary to build up such legends, and to enhance the reputation of the well for healing. Another part of the legend says that St Augustine vanquished 'Heil', the pagan idol of the villagers, who drove Augustine and his followers out, attaching cows' or fishes' tails to their clothes. This gave rise to the local superstition, current up to the 18th century, that Cerne people had tails, as a result of their treatment of St Augustine!

William of Malmesbury's story, written in 1125, probably came nearer the truth. He tells how St. Edwold, a member of the Mercian Royal family, became a holy man and in a vision was told to go to the 'Silver Well' at Cerne. Later he gave some silver coins to a shepherd who gave him bread and water. The shepherd took him to the well, which Edwold immediately recognised from his dream — he built a small hermitage and lived by the well until his death in 871 AD.

Down the centuries, the reputation of the Silver Well continued to grow in three different forms. First, it was an 'oracular' well, for it was said that those who looked in the well on Easter morning would see apparitions of all those who would die within the year. Secondly it was a wishing well, where girls could drink and putting their hand on one of the stones, which appears to have a (St Catherine) wheel carved on it, wish for a husband. Thirdly, the well was for healing. Barren women who drank the water would become pregnant and the water was also good for generally improving the health and as a specific for sore eyes. It was also said that new-born babies should be dipped into the water just as the sun's rays first touch the surface, for the well directly faces the rising sun.

Dorothy Gardiner in her *Companion into Dorset* gives a good description of the well, written in 1937, but still accurate ....

"Under the tile-roofed churchyard wall, a path leads, dropping steeply, to fabled St. Augustine's Well. Eleven trees for the eleven Apostles are said to mark the approach; I counted 9 limes well on in years, a yew many-stemmed, and a great beech. There is a patch of very ancient walling behind this Silver Well of hermit Eadwald's retreat. Hart's tongue ferns droop over it, and mossy stones border it; the water, crystal clear, flows away perpetually through a miniature conduit, and after feeding the mill-pond, comes up at a well-head lined with old masonry and new in the main street"...

The writer goes on to quote the well-known spell for this well ... "Pluck a laurel leaf growing nearby; make it into a little cup and dip it in the well; then stand and face the Church and drink the miraculous water, wish, but silently and in secret, and in time you shall have your heart's desire".

The Silver Well remains much as Dorothy Gardiner described it, but for the fact that I counted only nine trees around the well. A sign gives the legend and states that up to the earlier part of this century, the well provided the drinking

The Silver Well, Cerne Abbas

water for Abbey Street in the village.

When the great Abbey was in existence, with the bustling town of Cerne around it, this must indeed have been a religious centre of some importance. That is why the presence of the virile Giant on the hill seems so incongruous and one cannot help wondering why the monks tolerated him. Local legends about the Giant are many, some say he was a fearsome ogre, captured and staked out by the village people on the hill, others that he was the Roman god Hercules. Another source suggests that a holy man, perhaps Augustine, was indeed met with a hostile reception in the village, had mud thrown at him, and went to clean himself up at the well. Here he suddenly spotted the great figure on the hill and cried out, "I see God!", meaning the pagan god, Heil. An attractive theory, but if it is meant to be taken literally, it will not do — for the Giant cannot be seen from the well. Another legend says that the Giant comes down to drink at the millstream when he hears the clock strike twelve.

There are other things in the village which give rise to speculation about pagan survivals, for instance the face on the left side of the church porch, with a great round mouth used as a flue — also the small yellow face with its tongue poking out, high up on one of the South windows inside the church.

There are many other holy wells in Dorset, including 'Stachy's Well' at Ibberton, a 'Holy Well' near Evershot, St. Andrew's Well near Bridport, and the famous 'wishing-well' at Upwey. Most of these would have existed in pagan times, and would have had pagan legends attached to them, but as elsewhere, they would have been 'Christianised' in Anglo-Saxon times and re-dedicated to Christian saints.

The Wishing Well at Upwey 1900

Grottoes and Follies

Incongruous among a development of luxury residences and close by an old corner of Swanage where upturned boats and piles of fishing nets still litter the foreshore, stands a tall Gothic clock tower — looking as if it should belong to a church. But there is no church, nor clock, only the tower, looking, as Treves described it, 'finicking, elegant and townish'. This edifice once graced London Bridge where it had been a memorial to the Duke of Wellington. It was removed in 1863 and brought to Swanage to join various other oddities which were sent from afar to beautify the town. A couple of sons of the town had made good on the streets of London and, at various intervals they sent London street-signs, stone facades, and even a set of cannonballs back to Swanage. The cannonballs were to commemorate the defeat of the Danes by King Alfred in the year 877 AD, some 400 years before the invention of gunpowder!

Most 'follies' were not transported whole from another site as this one was, but were usually built, often at great expense, in the patron's own grounds — to show he had 'more money than sense' some would say. For the true definition of a folly must be that it really is of no use for anything at all — indeed the dictionary definition is "a ridiculous thing".

The tallest folly in Dorset is the 120 foot high tower in the grounds of Charborough Park, just visible from the road, for the grounds are not open to the public. This was built to an octagonal design in 1796 and is in a style usually described as 'Strawberry Hill Gothic'. The tower is featured in Hardy's *Two on a Tower*. Horton Tower is a huge ugly red-brick structure now beginning to crumble. It is also known as 'Sturt's Folly' and was built by Humphrey Sturt in the mid-18th Century as a watch-tower for the deer-park, but was left unfinished. It is seven stories high and has a fireplace halfway up, which cannot now be reached as the steps have now succumbed to time and the elements.

A smaller tower in an even worse state of repair is the round tower on the cliff overlooking Kimmeridge Bay. Built in a mixture of architectural styles, it has Gothic window openings and a Gothic handrail around the top, but is encircled by a Doric colonnade on the outside. Treves calls it a 'ridiculous tower'. If it has to have a purpose and surely no true folly should, then judging from its position, it might have served as a look-out tower. The 'Philosopher's Tower' which stands just off the Cranborne to Wimborne Road by the turning to Woodlands, is a much more attractive building. It was apparently built by a local landowner as a place of retreat. Boasting two stories, each consists of a single small room with a fireplace. Wooden stairs connects the two rooms. On top of Weatherbury Castle, which is on the road from Milborne Stileham to Turner's Puddle, is a brick tower in the form of a classical column with a ball-shape on top. Creech Grange Arch on the Isle of Purbeck, not far from Church Knowle, was built in 1746 by Denis Bond of Creech Grange, whose family gave their name to Bond Street in London. It comprises three medieval-style arches of Portland stone and was apparently built to enhance the view from the house.

Grottoes were made fashionable by Capability Brown, who, in the 18th century, in a frenzy of almost religious zeal, swept away all traces of

The Philosopher's Tower, near Woodlands

formal gardens and shaped flower beds, to form natural-looking landscapes of rolling parkland with groups of carefully planted trees. Little caves and grottoes with natural water-sources running through them were all the rage and few parks were without such attractions. In Dorset a few remain.

In the grounds of Wimborne St Giles House, is a 'Shell Grotto' made in 1751 by a temperamental Italian garden designer who would let no one watch him work. The shells came from India and the Caribbean and it was apparently more of an attempt to create an underwater room, with flints, fossils and pieces of minerals embedded in the surrounding walls. The whole thing was said to have been ruinously expensive and eventually cost thousands of pounds. Charborough Park also had a grotto, once an ice-house in which certain conspirators plotted the dethronement of James II.

Most extraordinary circumstances surround the set of 'mock ruins' in the grounds of Milton Abbey, for it was here in 1786 that the "unmannerly, imperious" Lord Milton, demolished the entire old town of Middleton, to improve his view from the new Manor House which had taken the place of the ancient monastic buildings. He built a set of mock ruins from the stones of perfectly good buildings which he had torn down. The Rev. Herbert Pentin gave a detailed description of how these ruins were constructed — to a more or less cruciform shape, with several arched windows of the 'pointed' style. He described the "lofty octagonal pinnacles" and the incised cross which decorated the East wall. Naturally the ruin was never roofed, and when Pentin described it in 1904, the shape was obscured by rampant ivy. He remarked on its much delapidated state, commenting drily ...

"May it, however, long stand as one of the monuments of that remarkable man who, though he destroyed a town, erected a ruin."

Kimmeridge Tower

The Twelve Days of Christmas

Bringing in the 'back-brand' or Yule Log

In the traditional Mummer's play good St. George (or King George) always slays the evil dragon or a fierce Turkish Knight. The hero is then revived by the 'magic' of the Medicine Man or Doctor, and the forces of evil are vanquished once again.

So runs the traditional theme of the age-old mummers' play, which still survives in some places, usually performed during the Christmas period. The theme can be said to epitomise the basis of all our traditional winter festivals — which almost all originate from the idea of the forces of Light overcoming the Dark. The mummers' plays vary but the message is always the same. The plays were not written down, but were handed down orally from generation to generation, because of the insistence on the idea that nothing must be changed or the 'magic won't work'. As a result the dialogue has become somewhat garbled over the centuries.

All the great fire festivals of the winter originate in this same idea, and many can be traced back to the influence of the Norse invaders — for 'Yule' was the name of their mid-winter celebration. They brought with them the Yule log, the legends of the mistletoe and the tales of St Nicholas, believed to be derived from the tales of the Norse god Woden, who rode across the sky in his chariot bearing gifts.

The Yule log was an important part of the Christmas celebration for country folk. Brought in on Christmas Eve, it was sometimes so large that it took half a dozen men to get it into the house. Sometimes called the 'back-brand' in this part of the country and sometimes taking the form of a number of ashen faggots, bound tightly together,

it was the subject of some superstitious practice. The log must be kept burning all through the twelve days of Christmas, for maximum good fortune. Then a small piece of the embers must be kept to light next year's fire. The presence of this ember in the house was believed to be a protection against fire for the coming year. The piece was taken out and burned for a short time on Candlemas Day (February 2nd), then doused and put away again till next Christmas Eve.

The twelve-day Roman 'Saturnalia' seems to have been the origin of the idea of 'twelve days of Christmas'. In Roman times all manner of celebrations took place and the usual order of things was turned upside down as masters waited on their servants. The birthday of the old Sun-god, Sol Invictus, the inconquerable sun, was celebrated at this time, for it was not until the 4th century that Christ's birthday was fixed on the 25th December.

Christmas Eve has long been considered the start of the festive season, when preparations were made for the days of feasting to follow. Mince pies could be eaten for the first time today, and ideally one should be eaten on each of the twelve days, preferably partaking of each one in a different house. Bread baked on Christmas Eve was said never to go mouldy, for the forces of evil were thought to be powerless on this holy day. Many people believed that at midnight the cattle would kneel in their stalls just as they did in their stable at Bethlehem. Decorations were put up on this day, with holly and other greenery, and mistletoe for kissing under, a custom which has the oldest origins of all, being descended from a Celtic fertility rite. In Dorset the 'gleemen', or 'wassailers' would come round singing carols, as they did in

The 'King of the Bean' at the Twelfth Night feast

Of Back-Brands, Mummers and Merrymaking

Hardy's *Under the Greenwood Tree*, later being rewarded with hot spiced ale from the wassail bowl.

Children everywhere knew that Father Christmas would come, bringing good things if they hung up their stockings by the chimney. This custom is derived from an old story about the Christian Saint Nicholas and is one which shows no sign whatever of dying out.

And so the feasting and merriment would continue throughout the twelve days with little but essential work being done. Country folk ate rich foods, such as roast goose and plum porridge. We are given an insight into the celebrations of the 'gentry' in the *Journal of Mary Frampton* published in 1885. Mary Frampton was a member of the prominent Dorset family ..

> "Our Christmas passed with a large family party at Moreton. The house was unbarred and unblockaded, with the exception of one large window on the staircase. The carol singers from Mr Frampton's own parishes ushered in Christmas Eve and Christmas morn as usual, but no mummers were allowed to perform their ancient drama of the wonderful recovery of a man killed in battle, by a little bottle of elixir drawn from the pocket of the Doctor of the piece ....
>
> The Yule log, however, burnt on the large hearth of the entrance hall. The peacock in full plumage, with its fiery mouth, was placed on the dinner table, with, of course, the boar's head; the immense candles were well covered with laurel, the hare appeared with a red herring astride on its back; and the wassail bowl and lamb's wool were not inferior to former years."

Twelfth Night saw the end of the festive period, but it went out with a 'Bang' and the best party of all. A King and a Queen were chosen for the night, by means of a cake containing a pea and a bean. The ale flowed freely and there were riotous games, singing and dancing far into the night. The mummers went round to perform their plays at all the larger houses and games and forefeits were enjoyed by all.

After Twelfth Night came Plough Monday and a return to work on the land, with 'Blessing the Plough' ceremonies which marked the beginning of another farming year. Last year's corn dolly was ploughed into the soil and the plough-boys would parade around the streets, while the ladies went back to their spinning.

The Mummers, complete with the Turkish Knight, St George and the Doctor

Conjuring Minterne

The crooked pinnacle on the Church tower

In a field by Batcombe Church, there is a spot where the grass never grows — for as local legend tells, here the horse of the weird Squire of Batcombe landed, after taking a flying leap, clean over the top of the church tower!

In this far corner of Dorset, down a steep and sudden hill, the tiny hamlet of Batcombe nestles into the wooded skirts of Batcombe Hill. In this remote and untouched corner of the county, high-banked lanes wind on for endless miles, in primrose-studded, leafy splendour, the hedges a tangled avenue of honeysuckle and tall hazel bushes — the looming hill a densely packed mass of broad-leaved trees. There is little to show that this was a village, for all that remains is a farmhouse or two, a few cottages and a church. Precipitous lanes drop down from the crest of the hill, from the top of which can be seen magnificent views across the Blackmore Vale. On the top road is the mysterious pillar, the Cross-in Hand, upon whose origins many have speculated. Some sources suggest it may date back to pagan times, others more mundane, that it was simply a boundary marker. The pillar features in *Tess of the D'Urbevilles* as a 'swearing stone', while others believe it was the scene of a murder. In Hardy's poem, *The Lost Pyx*, he retells the medieval legend of the priest who was called to the deathbed of a man who lived some miles away. When the priest reaches the house of the dying man, he finds that he has lost the sacred pyx, containing the Holy Sacrament. He re-traces his steps and to his amazement is directed to the spot by a shaft of heavenly light beaming down where the lost pyx lies. All around in silent adoration, are the creatures of the forest all kneeling side by side.

After this miracle the spot was marked by the stone pillar, the Cross-in-Hand.

From the wind-swept top of the hill, it is possible to look down on the flat top of Batcombe church tower. Here the mind begins to play strange tricks, for one of the pinnacles surmounting the four corners of the tower is slightly crooked, and one calls to mind the strange tale of a local figure who was said to have dealings with the Devil. The story was that the Squire of Minterne, known locally as 'Conjuring Minterne' liked to dabble in the 'black arts' in his spare time. He was said to have performed many extraordinary feats, yet none so strange as that which occurred on a certain day when he set out on horseback over Batcombe Hill. Suddenly he remembered that he had left his book of magic spells open on the table, and fearing that his servants might take to meddling, he decided to pop back and put the book away. Instead of merely turning his horse around, the magician spurred on the horse, causing it to take a massive leap, right over the top of Batcombe church tower. As he sailed over, the horse's hooves caught one of the pinnacles and knocked it off. Naturally, it was widely suspected that he must have had some help from the 'Evil One'. The broken pinnacle was not restored until about a hundred years later, and it was replaced rather badly, for to this day, one pinnacle appears 'out of true'. In another version, the local people said that the Devil himself, mounted on horseback, had knocked it off when jumping over the church to show his scorn for it — and that to replace the pinnacle would bring down his anger upon them, which was their explanation as to why the piece of stone lay on the ground for so long

The Crackpot Squire of Batcombe

before being repaired.

This eccentric character continued to astound the local people right up to the time of his death, for he instructed, like Sir Anthony Ettricke, of Wimborne, that he should be buried "neither in the church nor out of it". At Wimborne this was carried out by placing Ettricke's tomb in the wall, but here a tomb was constructed which literally stood half inside the church and half outside. This part of the church no longer exists, so there is merely an odd-looking half-tomb in the church-yard. It is encrusted with lichen and crumbling and unfortunately any inscription it may have had is no longer decipherable. An odd memorial for an odd man. There are two plaques inside the church, dedicated to two different John Min-ternes, one dated 1592, and the other 1716, but it is not certain if either of these is our friend 'the conjuror'.

Inside, the church is rather plain, except for a most attractive screen made from golden Hamstone bringing a touch of brightness into the gloom. The church is dedicated to St Mary and has a 15th century castellated tower, surmounted by the famous pinnacles. Built from flint and the local Ham Hill sandstone, it has been carefully restored and sits in its grassy churchyard, in the quietest surroundings it is possible to imagine. Nonetheless, it is not too difficult to link the strange legend of 'Conjuring Minterne' with the mysterious pillar on top of the hill whose faint markings cannot be deciphered, and whose origins are as much of a mystery as they ever were.

Conjuring Minterne's half-tomb

The Cross-in-Hand on Batcombe Hill

Here's to Thee – Old Apple Tree

A good crop of apple blossom means a good year for cider.

On Old Twelfth Night, in parts of Dorset and neighbouring Somerset, strange fertility rites once took place in the apple orchard. The custom of 'wassailing', which still survives in one or two parts of Somerset, was an essential part of the year's work for those farmers whose prosperity depended on the cider apple. In rites which had more than a hint of primitive tree-worship about them, great fires were lit in the orchards, guns were fired through the branches of the trees and cider was poured on the ground around the tree roots. Finally, cider-soaked sops were placed in the branches of the trees as an offering to the tree-spirits. The participants, comprising all members of the family, with even the bed-ridden being carried out to join in the celebration, consumed much cider, sang special wassailing songs and generally had a riotous evening.

The ancient origins of the elements of these rites are not hard to spot. The Romans had a goddess of the apple trees called Pomona, and the offerings to her and other tree-spirits would have been a regular feature of worship. The libations of cider poured on the ground would give back to the tree some of its fruitfulness from last season, ensuring good crops for the next. The fires and the noise would serve to drive away evil spirits and the songs were clearly designed to ensure a good crop next year ...

> "Here's to thee, old apple tree,/Whence thou may'st bud and whence thou may'st blow;/Hats full, caps full, bushel baskets, sacks full,/And all my pockets full, too. Hooray!"
>
> Old wassailing song ... Somerset

Sometimes the fields, the cattle-sheds and the beehives were 'wassailed' too to ensure all-round prosperity. For many superstitious beliefs tended to attach to the main sources of income for country folk. It was considered to be courting disaster to fell apple trees and other crops would not grow anyway, where apples had been chopped to make way for them. It was a bad omen if the tree blossomed out of season and blossom and fruit together on the tree was much feared as an evil omen. Country people believed that the apples were not fit to eat until after St Swithun's day on July 15th. Some said the apples were 'christened' on St Peter's day, June 29th.

The amount of apple blossom was crucial in determining whether there would be a good crop. An old legend about St Dunstan explains why there are often a few days of frost around the time of his feast day on May 19th, at a time when the blossom is most vulnerable. The story was that Dunstan, when he was Abbot of Glastonbury was selling beer of his own brewing in the town. He sold his soul to the Devil in return for the promise of a few days' late frost, which would kill off the local apple blossom. This would later give rise to a shortage of cider, so that people would have to buy his beer instead!

If the apple crop was good then there would be plenty of cider too, and in the strongholds of English cider-making the success of the crop is still as important as ever. Somerset is the county best known for its 'Scrumpy', as it is called locally, but there is still a flourishing industry in Dorset, Devon, Hereford and Gloucestershire. Up to the early years of this century, most farmers had a few trees to produce their own cider — for gallons of cider were actually part of the men's wages.

Cider-press in use at Hinton St Mary about 1895.

Cider-Making traditions in Dorset

My Uncle, Stan Bartlett, remembers only too well how as a nine-year old boy, he lost his leg by getting tangled in the horse-driven cider press on a Trent farm.

Cider is made from crushed apples left to ferment without any other additives. There are still a few who make small quantities in the old-fashioned way, with a huge wooden press, containing a 'cheese' of crushed apples held in wads of sacking or straw. In autumn, just over the border in Somerset, the scent of apples still hangs heavy in the air around the orchards. Each grower has his favourite varieties; I remember as a child, stealing small, hard cider apples which turned out to be not at all suitable for eating. My aunt used to grow a variety called 'Sheep's Noses', a cider variety which I have been unable to find in any reference book.

The many varieties we know today have been developed since the Norman Conquest, in a 900-year long hybridisation process which began with the original wild crab-apple and which has resulted in a huge range of different types.

It is believed that the French monks who built Forde Abbey on the Somerset/Dorset border were the first to make cider in this country and that the growth in its popularity coincided with the spread of the Cistercian monasteries across the English countryside in the 12th and 13th centuries.

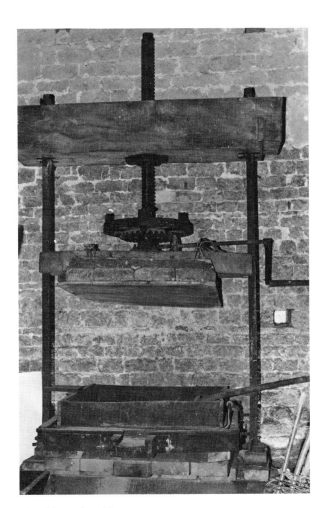

An old wooden cider press.

High Days and Holidays

'Guy Faux' carried in procession through the streets

For those who failed to take down the green Christmas decorations by Candlemas Day (February 2nd) great misfortune lay waiting in the year ahead. All the evergreens should be burned with only one last sprig of holly being kept to hang in the cowshed to give protection to the cattle. In pre-Reformation times, Candlemas was an important festival, with candle-lit processions in the church. For the day was the feast of the Purification of the Virgin Mary. Mothers who bore a child within the last year were blessed at this service.

In Lyme Regis it is said that most families sold their wood-ash throughout the year to an ash-man. He sent as a present, a large candle to every householder for Candlemas Day. This was lit on the day, with a good deal of merriment and ale-supping, which did not stop until the candle was finished. A small piece of the candle was kept till next year as a form of household protection.

On St. Valentine's Day, a Dorset custom was to hang a small bunch of early Spring flowers in the house, tied with a blue ribbon. Popular belief was that the birds choose their mates on this day and consequently there were various means by which girls sought to identify their future husbands. As everywhere, the sending of Valentine cards was well-developed by the last century.

Mothering Sunday or Mid-Lent Sunday was originally a church festival, when people working away from home would return to their 'mother-church' — paying a visit to their families at the same time. Simnel cake was the traditional dish for the day, and also 'furmity' or 'frumenty', made from steeped wheat, milk, currants and spices all boiled together.

The second Monday and Tuesday after Easter were known as 'Hock-tide' a season noted for various customs, such as the strange 'Tutti-men' who preside at an ancient ceremony in Hungerford, Berks. In Dorset the custom known as 'hocking' was prevalent, as in several other southern counties. This consisted of blocking the way with ropes and barriers and compelling members of the opposite sex to pay a forfeit for their right of passage. The men barred the women's way on Monday and the tables were turned on the Tuesday. The money thus collected went to local worthy causes. There are records of 'hocking' in Blandford going back to 1604.

St George's Day was celebrated in Dorchester and also in any village having the name St George. In neighbouring Somerset, at Hinton St. George, the children always had a day off school on the 23rd April.

They had another day off on May 29th, Oak Apple Day, for this was an important holiday. The children would sing ...

"It's Oak Apple Day, Oak Apple Day,
If you don't give us a holiday
We'll all run away"

The origin of this celebration was the Restoration of King Charles II in 1660, for it was also called Royal Oak Day, on account of his supposedly being found hiding in the Boscobel Oak. Houses were decorated with oak branches at least up to the early 19th Century. Any householder who did not deck his house with oak branches was liable to have his doorway decorated for him, with a bunch of nettles! The young men wore sprigs of oak leaves in their caps and saved up their pennies to buy one or two special leaves, made of

St George and the dragon, the stuff of fairytales

'real' gold leaf, to be added to the green ones. In parts of Somerset and Dorset the day was called 'Shick-shack day', though it is not clear why this should be so. In Wiltshire the celebration of certain woodland rights also took place at this time and the wearing of oak leaves was remembered as recently as 1902, when the carters attached sprigs of leaves to their horses' bridles.

'Guy Faux' day was very popular in Dorset as elsewhere, with every town and village putting on amusements and processions. As always there were disturbances of the peace and Udal speaks of an occasion about 1880 when the military had to be called out "in order to assist the civil authorities in the quelling of riots". He says there were "bonfires and flying fireworks" all over the county. At Marnhull in 1908 a torchlight procession with a band paraded round the village. There were all sorts of characters in costume, with decorated carts and cycles, and even a representation of 'Old Nick'. Guy Fawkes was ceremoniously hoisted to the top of the bonfire and burnt, amid much cheering. In Portland, fathers carried or led their children round the fire then each man, carrying a child, leapt through the flames. Later the children jumped over the dying embers. Once again it seems that in Portland, the memory of ancient custom survives longer than elsewhere, for here there are links with the pagan rites of human sacrifice.

Near Christmas, on St Thomas' Day, 21st December, up to the early years of this century, many children took the day off school to go 'gooding' or 'Christmasing'. This was done by the poorer families who would visit in turn, the houses of more well-off people, to obtain some goodies and sweetmeats for their Christmas feast.

Clearly village life in former times was far from dull — almost every month had its festivals and feast days, either secular or Christian — giving some opportunity for fun and feasting and perhaps a little drinking! Most workers had no annual holidays, so a day off was to be enjoyed to the full.

Apple-bobbing on Hallowe'en

No Moon No Man

Dorset's greatest writer, Thomas Hardy

Hardy's unrivalled reputation can be said to hinge on his deep understanding and knowledge of the county of Dorset combined with the hinterland of Old Wessex. His characterisation and insight into the lives of ordinary people and his awareness of the contemporary culture is unsurpassed. His supreme command of language reaches a peak in the description of Egdon Heath as the glowering backdrop for the most elemental of his works, *The Return of the Native*. In building his plots and setting his scenes he makes much use of omens and prophetic signs to point the reader's way and it is this insight into country lore which make the characters in his novels so satisfactory. That they are flesh and blood is beyond doubt, that they dwell in Hardy's Dorset is also beyond doubt for they are steeped in the ways and customs of the time. One can immediately recognise the hidden knowledge which is inherent in every culture.

Country folk of 150 years ago were plain and simple people, not many of them literate, but wise in country matters and in affairs of daily life. Their beliefs were a mixture of straightforward God-fearing christianity, with more than a dash of surviving pagan belief and age-old superstition. The Age of Science had not yet come — witness the mention in *Tess of the D'Urbervilles* of a 'Cunning-man' who would "cast folks' water" as a means of predicting the future. Divination was much in vogue, the old custom of sowing hemp-seed on Old Midsummer Eve was well-known as a means of finding out who a future husband might be. This practice occurs in *The Woodlanders* while in *Under the Greenwood Tree*, Mrs Penny describes her vision, brought about by another method....

"... never was I in such a taking as on that Midsummer Eve! I sat up, quite determined to see if John Wildway was going to marry me or no. I put the bread and cheese and cider, quite ready, as the witch's book ordered, and I opened the door, and I waited till the clock struck twelve, my nerves all alive, and so distinct that I could feel everyone of 'em twitching like bell-wires. Yes, sure! and when the clock had struck, lo and behold! I could see through the door a little small man in the lane wi' a shoe-maker's apron on."

Divination using the Bible and a key is found in *Far from the Madding Crowd*.

Superstitions are scattered everywhere in Hardy's books, some of Christian origin, such as the legend of the oxen kneeling at midnight on Christmas Eve, mentioned in *Tess* and in a poem simply called *The Oxen*; also in *A Changed Man* is the belief that God christens the apples on St Swithun's Day. Other superstitions are definitely of pagan origin, such as the expression 'pixy-led', meaning a person who gets lost by being bewitched by fairies. Such sayings express the common fear of the power of witches and fairies, centuries after the established Church forbade such beliefs. Many superstitions were attached to farm work and life. In *Tess* we see that the cows were said to withhold their milk if there was a new hand in the dairy and also that the butter would not 'come' if someone working there was in love.

Moon worship goes back much further than the beginning of Christianity, and yet remnants of it were still commonplace in the mid-1800s,

Butter will not 'come' if someone in the dairy is in love

as Hardy described in *The Well-beloved*, where he mentioned "bowing three times to the Moon"; also in *Jude the Obscure*, mention is made of 'praying to the Moon'. In *Return of the Native*, the reason given for Christian Cantle's disappointing masculinity, was that he was born when there was no moon — "No Moon — no man", was the verdict of his friends.

Signs and portents are found everywhere in Hardy's work — to break a key was an ominous piece of bad luck, found in *Far from the Madding Crowd*, and in the same book the old superstition about seeing a lone magpie is mentioned. One of the worst omens was to hear a crock crowing at midday, as Tess did before her fateful wedding day.

The most extreme cases of belief in witchcraft are the blatant examples of witch practice found in Hardy's work. Wax effigies appear both in *The Mayor of Casterbridge* and in *Return of the Native*. Here, Susan Nonsuch made an effigy of Eustacia Vye, for she believed that Eustacia had bewitched her son, making him ill; she fashioned the figure carefully, then stuck many pins into it and held it in the fire, all the while making a strange incantation, the Lord's Prayer backwards — known to be a most potent charm when spoken by a witch. Susan also pricked Eustacia in church with a long hatpin as a means of negating her supposed power.

In *Tess* appears the ghostly coach of the D'Urbervilles, which could only be seen by a person of the true family blood. This tale has a basis in fact, in as much as ghost stories can have a base in fact. Perhaps the best illustration of how folklore actually develops and accumulates, is Mrs Cantel's description in *The Dynasts* of the 'archogre' Napoleon's eating habits ....

> "I can tell you a word or two on't. It is about his victuals. They say that he lives upon human flesh, and has rashers of baby every morning for breakfast — for all the world like the Cernel Giant in ancient times."

This linking of Napoleon to the great symbol of the darker side of Dorset, the Cerne Giant, bridges the centuries and shows how even the most far-fetched tales can live on and attract further accretions from century to century. That Hardy could draw together all these diverse elements and weave them into the behaviour patterns of his characters is a recurring reminder of his genius in creating a convincing and enthralling 'genre'.

The Bockhampton cottage where Hardy was born

The Devil in Dorset

When a chapel was being built at Haythorne near Woodlands the work suddenly stopped, for it was declared that the Devil himself had entered the building, to interfere with the Lord's work. He could not be got out for several weeks, and the work could not proceed. Eventually he was driven out by a group of people who sang, shouted and hooted as loudly as they could, for to make a great deal of noise was thought to be the surest way to get rid of evil spirits.

In the Middle ages the Devil was a very potent force in the everyday lives of simple uneducated folk. They liked their religion to be graphic, for few could read — and churches were filled with colourful murals and images to bring home the Christian message. The devil would get you if you were wicked, and naturally tales grew up about the 'Evil One', who seemed to be lurking around every corner. Grotesque images on churches may have represented Satan, or may have been used in an attempt to scare him away. It was believed that witches were handmaidens of the Devil, and also that giants, fairies and other spirit-forms did his bidding. Anyone who dabbled in the occult or magic was said to be in league with the Devil. The Church leaders were paranoid about anything that could be construed as 'Devil-worship', hence the witch persecutions of the 17th century.

Devil legends are found all over the world but Dorset has a few of its own. One of the most common themes in this type of story concerns the Devil hurling rocks about, which then lie for many centuries, never losing their evil connotations. One such story refers to the Agglestone Rock at Studland. The legend is related by the historian Charles Warne in *Notes and Queries* ...

"country people say ... that his Satanic majesty (who is often a very important personage in these capricious freaks) was one day sitting on the Needles Rock, Isle of Wight, whence, espying Corfe Castle in the distance, he took the cap from his head and threw it across the sea, with the intent of demolishing that structure. But it would appear that he had over-estimated his powers of jactation, for the missile fell short of its mark, and there it stands to this day on Studland Heath, a monument of disappointed malice, a wonder to the peasantry, and a theme of antiquarian conjecture."

Hence its local name, 'The Devil's Night-cap' derived from the shape of the rock which is a sort of inverted cone, some 17 feet high and about 35 feet in diameter. An extension to this legend says that the Devil also threw some smaller stones, which landed at Rempstone, halfway between Studland and Corfe. One source says that the name 'Agglestone' is derived from the Saxon 'Haligstan', meaning 'Holy Stone', which could point to some early significance in religious ceremony. Another eminent writer, F.J.Harvey Darton says that the 'stories told by scientists are less interesting and not much more plausible'.

The Hell-stone near Portesham was said to have been thrown by the Devil from Portland where he was playing quoits, while near Lambert's Castle, between Thorncombe and Marshwood there are three clumps of trees on small hillocks. These are known as 'The Devil's Jumps', for it was said that the Devil was kicked out of Forde Abbey by the Abbot and bounced three times on the way to Birdsmoor gate. The 'Devil's

The Devil's Nightcap, Agglestone Rock, near Studland

Old Harry's Impact on the Landscape

Brook' runs through Dewlish and Burleston and the famous 'Old Harry Rocks' at Swanage are also named after Satan, 'Old Harry' being a favourite pseudonym. Other local names for the Devil include 'the very old 'un', 'Owld lad', also 'Old Nick' or 'Old Scratt' and so on. These are often found in the nicknames of well-known plants, such as 'Devil's Peascods' for laburnum, which is poisonous, 'Devil's Snuff-box' for the puffball, and 'Devil's Guts' for the wild clematis. 'The Devil's Bird' was the magpie, long thought to have evil powers.

'His Satanic majesty' is linked with many other tales in Dorset, for instance, the black horse which gathered with all the other animals around the shaft of light shining on the 'Lost Pyx' in Hardy's poem, refused to kneel — for he was the Devil in disguise. His purpose was to trick men into trying to ride him, so that he could then obtain power over them. In an ancient barn in French Mill Lane, Shaftesbury, young men would gather on Sundays to play cards, which was forbidden by the Church. One Sunday a stranger appeared to join the game but as he played he dropped a card and accidentally showed a cloven hoof to his companions. Needless to say, they were so alarmed that the Sunday gambling was discontinued.

Old Harry Rocks, near Swanage

Medieval Markets

John Horner of Charlton Marshall, off to Blandford Market in 1880

"Shaftesbury has more strong beer than water ..."

This was surely borne out on Market Days in the Middle Ages, when the normally drowsy little town became a bustling, roaring, unruly, teeming mass of excited humanity — coming in for the day from the fields and villages, stopping off at every tavern along the way. In the narrow, crowded streets, there was a tavern on every corner and down every alley-way, and no shortage of customers, for Shaftesbury's beer was well-known for its strength.

In the Middle Ages, life for country folk was often isolated — communication was difficult and the supply of daily needs a constant problem. But by the 13th century, development was beginning, with new boroughs being created. The need for disposing of and exchanging different commodities led to the growth of markets, which could only be granted by Royal Charter. Such Charters were granted to Blandford, Charmouth, Corfe, Lyme Regis, Melcombe Regis, Poole, Sherborne, Weymouth and Whitchurch Canonicorum, among other Dorset towns.

The weekly market system created a network of trade which was of vital importance to the rural economy and few places were so isolated that they did not have a market within 15 or 20 miles. Most markets were fairly modest affairs, serving the local districts, while a few became large specialist markets, serving customers from several counties, especially near the main areas of corn production, such as Shaftesbury, Salisbury and Warminster. In the early 17th century, a typical range of goods seen at local markets, apart from the animals, would have included butter, cheese, leather, vegetables, hops, wood and iron ware, cloth and wool. Chapmen and pedlars would also have been much in evidence, selling trinkets, ribbons and pins, or sweetmeats.

The typical market scene would have been a colourful, chaotic hubbub of noise and smells, the narrow streets filled with stalls, sellers and buyers all jostling for elbow room, drovers with their animals, tethered cattle and horses getting in the way, with stall-holders loudly crying their wares and farmers tipping out sacks of corn to show the quality. The country folk would have streamed in from all the surrounding villages to take part in the proceedings, and meet up with old friends.

At Cerne Abbas the farmers 'pitched' their samples of grain on the cobbles outside the row of ancient cottages facing the church, still known as 'Pitchmarket'. Cerne's market Charter was granted by King John in 1214 to the Abbot of Cerne, who would collect the tolls due from traders. The market here continued to thrive until the late 18th century, but the improved transport system, and later the railways failed to reach Cerne; good communications are the life-blood of markets, and so the market here gradually dwindled away. Dorchester and Blandford both had very busy markets, while at Sturminster Newton, still an important market town, sheep and pigs were held in pens along the main streets of the town and cattle and horses were tied to railings around the market place. The smaller markets tended to decline as road communications improved, meaning that people could travel further to get to the largest markets. Frampton

Mountebank selling his wares on Market Day

market was eclipsed by Dorchester, and at Bere Regis, Beaminster, Blandford and Bridport, fire or the plague hastened the decline, so that in the end only the major markets of Shaftesbury, Sturminster Newton and Dorchester had any real importance. At the end of the 19th Century Shaftesbury market almost disappeared because of competition from nearby Gillingham which had thrived on its railway. Later the day was changed, which solved the problem.

Shaftesbury was an important centre mainly because of its position between the hills and the Vale, on main roads from Bristol to Poole and London to Exeter. Great quantities of corn from the rich lands of the Blackmore Vale were sold here. Laura Sydenham, in her excellent study of *Shaftesbury and its Abbey*, mentions by name no less than 51 pubs, though clearly not all of these were operating at once. Certainly there would have been over 20 open at any one time to supply the market visitors with beer, much of which was brewed in the town. The Corn Market, described in 1620 as "a fair timber building with a bell in it", was probably situated in the centre of what is the present Cornmarket. The 'fish cross', of stone with a lead roof, stood on Gold Hill till 1780, selling fish and poultry. In 1562 a butter cross, or 'cheese cross', was built, which sold dairy produce and which confusingly was sometimes called 'the poultry cross' like the one in Salisbury. Cattle and pigs were sold on Gold Hill. (The name may be derived from the Saxon — 'Gelt', meaning payment)

The market Charter was first granted in 1260, with the rights to the tolls being held by the Abbey. In 1392 Richard II confirmed the grant of two markets to Shaftesbury, one on Mondays and one on Saturdays, as well as an extra one on Sundays between August and Michaelmas, to cover the harvest period. Even in those days it was a huge market and the tolls collected must have brought large amounts of revenue. After the dissolution of the Abbey this revenue came into the hands of various local people for in the course of normal business transactions the rights to tolls could be bought and sold like any other commodity.

Today, most of Dorset's larger towns still have weekly markets, though not all of them are of ancient origin. The large cattle market at Sturminster still exists and Wimborne has a huge three-day market combining an antique fair and stalls for modern 'gewgaws' — but these are surely only a pale imitation of the wonderful, noisy, smelly, crowded Market Days of old.

The 'Pitchmarket' at Cerne, where farmers pitched their corn samples

Ancient Networks of Trade and Commerce

Of Cabbages and Kings ...

The very first cabbage in this country was grown in the gardens of Wimborne St. Giles House. This astonishing claim to fame is only one of the stories attached to this fine house, seat of the Earls of Shaftesbury. In St Giles church the tomb of Sir Anthony Ashley, Earl of Shaftesbury, shows a ball-shape at his feet, said to be the very cabbage. Understandably such a rare delicacy was at first very expensive, one source says that in 1595 six cabbages cost 20 shillings, which was an outrageously large sum of money.

Among the numerous and far-ranging Dorset legends that survive are many of a 'fairy-tale' nature, such as the legend of the 'Giant's Grave' at Cheselbourne. This tells how two giants had a stone-throwing contest on the hill. The loser was so broken-hearted that he lay down and died of despair, and was buried under the stones. The valley of the Frome under Poundbury was once, so legend tells, a huge lake frequented by dragons and monsters, while at Lyme and at other locations in the county, the dreaded 'Black Dog' roamed the lonely lanes at dead of night. Others have written fully about the many ghosts of Dorset, especially the army of ghostly soldiers seen at Poyntington, and the team of fourteen ghosts which haunts Sandford Orcas Manor, not to mention the fairy of Purse Caundle. Those of nervous disposition should keep away from Trent Barrow, where there is a 'bottomless pool' into which a coach and horses once plunged. Neither driver, passengers, nor horses were ever seen again. Some say that passers-by on the roadway may hear upon the wind the galloping horses' hooves and the wailing of the dead. A pool in the Stour at Durweston has a similar reputation and is said to

harbour a horse and cart in its depths.

Some stories are attached to real people of Dorset, such as the curse of the Frampton family. There was once a monastery on the site of the Manor House, and when Henry VIII dissolved all the religious houses, the Abbot was naturally feeling aggrieved that the buildings would pass out of his hands, and laid a curse to the effect that the eldest son of every succeeding generation of the family would die before he was old enough to inherit his property. Certainly up to the 1920s that curse was fulfilled, no elder Frampton son lived to succeed the inheritance.

The Squire of Wynford Eagle was a 'bad lot'! The Manor came to the Sydenham family in 1551, from its original Norman owners who came from Aquila in Normandy — ('Aquila' means 'eagle') The most famous Sydenham was Thomas who became a great physician and is sometimes called the 'Father of English medicine' but the last of the family line brought disgrace upon the house. This was William Sydenham, who had severe financial problems. When pondering how best to solve them, he had what seemed like a brilliant idea. He decided to 'raffle' the Manor House. His plan included the co-opertion of a female confederate, a family friend. For a small sum she would upon receiving the winning ticket, by foul means of course, relinquish the house to its owner, who would of course pocket a handsome return from the sale of the lottery tickets. Unfortunately for him, the plan backfired and the woman friend refused to carry out her part of the bargain. The Squire and his daughters refused to move and the matter went to law. The Squire lost and languished nine years in jail before he died.

The symbolic 'cabbage' at the foot of Sir Anthony Ashley's tomb in Wimborne St Giles Church

Some Dorset Oddments

Other light-hearted tales of Dorset folk include the tale of the sometime Sherriff of Dorchester who thought it would be a good idea to let all prisoners out of jail and the rather tall tale that solemnly relates that the 'mayoralty' of Winterbourne Abbas goes to the next person who falls in the stream. This person keeps the title of Mayor, would you believe, until someone else falls in!

The story of the Dewlish Elephants is not a tall tale, for mammoth remains were indeed found at Dewlish. The creatures had tusks over six feet long and "molars like great lumps of rock" as one commentator puts it. The scientific name for these strange inhabitants of millennia past is 'elephas meridionalis', the 'elephant of the South', as it was popularly named. Apparently it lived when England was a much warmer place than it is now, but died out in the Pliocene Age. Other notable fossil remains include the many found at Charmouth and the strange 'fossil forest' above Lulworth Cove.

As for the Kings, down the long centuries Dorset has been host to royalty many times. The first, if legend has a grain of truth, was Boadicea, who is supposed to have been defeated by the Romans on Castle Hill at Cranborne. Most authorities dispute this and place the venue as Epping Forest, which is Dorset's loss. The legendary King Arthur was said to have won a bloody battle against the Saxons on Badbury Rings. Athelstan had many links with Dorset and is especially remembered for his founding of Milton Abbey. He was a great collector of holy relics and presented Milton with the arm of St Branwalader and many other bits of bone and precious relics. Alfred the Great founded the town of Shaftesbury with its great Abbey and his daughter Elgiva was the first Abbess. King John spent much time hunting at Tollard Royal on the border with Wiltshire and also in his parks at Gillingham. His daughter, Queen Joan of Scotland, was buried at Tarrant Crawford in the Cistercian Abbey, of which there is now no trace — while the heart of the Dane who became the English King, Cnut, was buried in Shaftesbury Abbey.

Charles II's jaunt around Dorset while he was 'on the run' is well known, but there is a less famous escapade at Wimborne St Giles House when the King got very drunk and knighted Edward Hooper of Boveridge, who it was said, received the honour "for keeping his head while losing his legs"! Lastly, the prominence of Weymouth as a seaside resort is put down to the enthusiasm with which, in 1789, George III or 'Fat George', plunged into the sea from a bathing-machine — to the strains of the National Anthem played by a brass band concealed in a similar hut!

George III bathing at Weymouth in 1789

Dorset's Deserted Villages

A few days before Christmas 1943, the two hundred and fifty inhabitants of Tyneham village left their homes so that their idyllic surroundings could be turned into a practice grounds for tanks. Others have written fully about this regrettable event and the greater sadness which followed, for the villagers were never able to return to their homes, as they had been promised. It is true that this beautiful area has become a haven for wildlife because of the restricted public access over the years — but sometimes people can be an endangered species too and the demise of a thriving community can only be described as a tragedy.

There have been many other 'deaths' of villages in Dorset. Only two are believed to have suffered a violent demise, these are Ringstead and West Bexington, both of which are said to have been destroyed by foreign raiders. In the case of Ringstead this is supposed to have happened in the 15th Century. Now only overgrown mounds and a few crumbling scraps of wall remain to show that there once was a living, breathing community here, though remains of a church in the form of a 13th century arch, incorporated in a cottage, were visible in Treves' time, together with two or three ancient cottages. The last rector of East Ringstead Church, John Whitacre, was installed in 1465 and apart from that known fact, there is no documentation explaining what happened to the tiny settlement. It was one of three linked hamlets, the others being West and Middle Ringstead. Ronald Good, in his book, *The Lost Villages of Dorset* lists forty-two deserted villages in the county, saying that the lowering of the water-table in chalk areas could have been one reason for the death of some villages. There are fewer 'lost' sites in the West and North of Dorset, probably because this area was always more sparsely populated, being mainly covered by forest.

One group of settlements was concentrated around the present village of Milborne St. Andrew. Hutchins listed the following ... M St.Andrew, M Stileham, M Deverel or Cary, M Churchstone, M Mamford, M Michaelston and M Sydmonston, most of which no longer exist. In recent years a large pasture called 'Culeaze' or 'Cowleaze', West of Weatherbury Castle hillfort has been found to contain the remains of a medieval village. This ten-acre field is also the site of the 'golden coffin' legend mentioned elsewhere in this book. The name of the village is not known, but Good believes it is Milborne Sydmonston and that it suffered its demise in the 14th or 15th Century.

Good also lists some eighty villages which are now reduced only to a farmhouse but which were once small settlements, some of which were first inhabited in Saxon times. He also lists a further twenty-six cases in which all that now remains is a Manor House.

Knowlton is an example of a village which has totally disappeared, also Gussage St Andrew — both of these now have only a Church, ruined in the case of Knowlton. Stanton St Gabriel's desolation seems to have been the result of a natural migration when the old coast road was superseded by a new turnpike. Belchalwell was a parish which was absorbed into two others and Mapperton was decimated by the plague in 1666. East Fleet is a coastal village which was swept away in the great storm of 1824, when the sea poured over the top of the Chesil Beach, washing away most of the

Vanished Communities and Lost Heritage

village leaving only the tiny chancel of the church standing. This still stands as a little chapel and a new church was built a little way inland.

The reasons for the abandonment or dwindling of villages are often complex and in many cases the actual causes are unknown. Besides the question of water-tables, there are several other important factors. Some old villages have simply become swallowed up as the larger towns have spread their boundaries outwards. This applies to villages like Kinson in Bournemouth and Chickerell in Weymouth. The enclosure of land would also have caused the dispersal of many small settlements as farming methods were rationalised and also the enclosure of common land meant that people often had to migrate to find work. Changes in roads and increased traffic would also have had a bearing, as the new turnpikes developed after 1750.

In earlier times the Plague was a major cause of drastic population loss. The disease first entered Dorset at Melcombe Regis in 1348 and soon decimated the local population. The monastic communities were very hard hit, especially the Cistercian houses, which relied on large numbers of lay-brothers to do the work of husbandry and farming. It is believed that the population of the country as a whole fell by between 30 and 50 per cent and many villages simply disappeared off the face of the earth. There was no-one to work the land. Once a village had been hit by plague, it was unlikely that the survivors if any, would return; there was understandably a reluctance to go back to a place where the memories were all bad, not to mention the fear of re-infection.

Another factor was the change of ownership and tenancy of properties. When a property was sold or split up, naturally this would affect the workers who lived in nearby settlements. After the Dissolution of the Monasteries there was much movement where confiscated property was sold off and shared out to Henry's supporters and the folk who worked for the Lord of the Manor were often dispossessed. Then there were a few deliberate clearances, like the clean sweep Lord Milton made of the old town of Middleton, for the sake of his view.

Ronald Good says that the main cause of depopulated villages seems to be a rise in the general population, since a small village cannot support large numbers of people, some of whom would have to migrate to the towns for work and accommodation. This trend has continued into the 20th century and was of course hastened by the Industrial Revolution which made drastic changes to the old way of English life.

Though we still have many lovely villages in Dorset, it is hard not to grieve for those which are lost. Many people's lives lie buried beneath the tangled weeds. Tread softly, for you tread on our past.

Tyneham now, a sad and desolate ruin

BIBLIOGRAPHY

Dorsetshire Folklore: J. S. Udal (Hertford, 1922); Highways and Byways of Dorset: Sir Frederick Treves (London, 1906); The Marches of Wessex: F. J. Harvey Darton (London, 1936); Shell Guide to Dorset: M. Pitt Rivers (London, 1966); Walking in Dorset: J. Begbie (London, 1936); The Lost villages of Dorset: R. Good (Wimborne, 1987); South Devon and Dorset Coast: S. Heath (London, 1910); Memorials of Old Dorset: T. Perkins and H. Pentin (London, 1907); Companion into Dorset: D. Gardiner (London, 1943); Dorset Upalong and Downalong: ed M. Dacombe (Dorchester, 1951); Shaftesbury and its Abbey: L. Sydenham (1959); Dorset: Arthur Mee (London, 1945); Dorset Curiosities: G. Osborne (Wimborne, 1988); Old Dorset: M. B. Weinstock (1967); Dorset Essays: Llewellyn Powys (1935); Trent in Dorset: A Sandison (Dorchester, 1969); Old Dorset: H. J. Moule (1893); Cerne Abbas: M. D. Jones (London, 1952); Chambers Book of Days — vols I and II (London 1864); Hone's Everyday Book — vols I and II (London, 1827); Hutchins' History of Dorset — 4 volumes (1774); Proceedings of the Dorset Natural History and Archaeologial Society (formerly the Natural History and Antiquarian Field Club) — from 1877; Somerset and Dorset Notes and Queries — from 1890; Dorset Year Books; Oral Folk Tales of Wessex: K Palmer (Newton Abbot, 1973); Church and Parish: J. H. Bettey (London, 1987); Roads and Trackways of Wessex: G. Wright (Ashbourne, 1988); Man At Play: J. Armitage (London, 1977).